Robert Williamson

Church Government and Church Questions

Robert Williamson

Church Government and Church Questions

ISBN/EAN: 9783743341531

Manufactured in Europe, USA, Canada, Australia, Japa

Cover: Foto ©Lupo / pixelio.de

Manufactured and distributed by brebook publishing software (www.brebook.com)

Robert Williamson

Church Government and Church Questions

CHURCH GOVERNMENT

AND

CHURCH QUESTIONS.

BY THE

REV. ROBERT WILLIAMSON,
ASCOG, ROTHESAY.

EDINBURGH: DUNCAN GRANT.
LONDON: JAMES NISBET & CO.
1869.

CONTENTS.

CHAPTER I.

ON THE IDENTITY OF PRESBYTERS AND BISHOPS.

PAGE

The Argument from Scripture—From the Early Fathers—From the English Reformers, and the Early English Church, ... 1

CHAPTER II.

The Ruling Elder—Subordination of Church Courts, . 29

CHAPTER III.

Argument from the Cases of Timothy, Titus, and the Angels of the Seven Churches of Asia, . . . 33

CONTENTS.

CHAPTER IV.

ON THE RIGHTS AND STANDING OF PRESBYTERS IN CON-
FERRING ORDINATION.

PAGE

The Doctrine of the Church of England—Of the Scotch Episcopal Church—Archbishops Sancroft, Wake, Secker, Usher, Potter, Howley; Bishops Morton, Cosin, Wordsworth, &c., ...   39

CHAPTER V.

IMPORTANT DIFFERENCE IN DOCTRINE BETWEEN THE COM-
MUNION OFFICE OF THE CHURCH OF ENGLAND AND THAT
OF THE SCOTCH EPISCOPAL CHURCH.

The Scotch Communion Office—The Invocation Prayer— Bishops Innes, Rattray, Jolly, Torry, Forbes, Skinner, Gleig—Debate in Convocation in 1862—The Bishops of Oxford, Lincoln, Llandaff, ...   51

CHAPTER VI.

SOURCES FROM WHICH THE SCOTCH COMMUNION OFFICE HAS
BEEN DERIVED.

The Missal—Fragmenta Liturgica—Principal Baillie—Hallam—Malcolm Laing—The Oriental Liturgies—The Greek Church, ...   70

CONTENTS. vii

CHAPTER VII.

THE REFORMED CHURCHES, AND THE DOCTRINE OF THE SACRAMENTS.

PAGE

The Scotch Confession of 1560—Craig's Catechism, 1592—Synod of London, 1552—Articles of the Church of England—Zwingle—Consensus Tigurinus—Cranmer—Ridley—Athanasius—Augustine—Communion Service of the Church of England for the Sick, . . 87

CHAPTER VIII.

ON APOSTOLICAL SUCCESSION.

No evidence in support of from Scripture—Succession of Doctrine, not of Persons, founded upon by the most eminent of the early Fathers, and the most distinguished Divines of the Church of England—Irenæus—Tertullian—Cyprian—Ambrose—Gregory Nazianzen—Augustine—Bradford—Jewell—Whitaker—Hoadly—Field—Stillingfleet—Whately, . . . 103

CHAPTER IX.

CONCLUSIONS ARRIVED AT.

Difference of Opinion among Episcopal Authors—Council of Trent—Provincial Assembly of London in 1653—Forbes of Carse—Bellarmine—Leighton's "Zion's Plea against Prelacy," 124

CHAPTER X.

THE DOCTRINE OF THE ROYAL SUPREMACY, AND THE SPIRITUAL
INDEPENDENCE OF THE CHURCH.

PAGE

Debates in the Westminster Assembly—Coleman—Lightfoot—Selden—Gillespie—The Thirty-Seventh Article of the Church of England—The Injunctions of Queen Elizabeth—The Irish Articles—Latimer—Cranmer—Usher—John Livingstone—Alexander Henderson—Sir Roundell Palmer—Dr Ball, . . . 130

APPENDIX, . . . 163

CHURCH GOVERNMENT AND CHURCH QUESTIONS.

CHAPTER I.

ON THE IDENTITY OF PRESBYTERS AND BISHOPS.

The Argument from Scripture—From the Early Fathers—From the English Reformers, and the Early English Church.

" What was not in the times of the Apostles cannot be deduced from them. We say in Scotland, 'It cannot be brought but that is not in the ben ;' but (not to insist on a liturgy, and things of that kind) there was no such hierarchy, no such difference betwixt a Bishop and a Presbyter in the times of the Apostles, and therefore it cannot hence be deduced ; for I conceive it to be as clear as if it were written with a sunbeam, that Presbyter and Bishop are to the Apostles one and the same thing ; no majority, no inequality or difference of office, power, or degree betwixt the one and the other, but a mere identity in all."

" Notwithstanding all that is pretended from antiquity, a Bishop having sole power of ordination and jurisdiction will never be found in prime antiquity."—*Alexander Henderson's Correspondence with Charles I.* Letters of date 3d June 1646, and 17th June 1646.

THE efforts at present being made to bring about an union of the Roman Catholic, Greek, and Anglican

Churches* are professedly based on the ground that these three bodies possess in common what they are pleased to call the "threefold order of the ministry," viz., Bishops, Presbyters or Priests, and Deacons; and that they alone have a "*Priesthood*" and a "*Sacrifice.*" In other words, their prelatic power as lords or governors in Christ's Church, and their priestly power, as alone authorised to administer the sacraments of the Church, are the two corner-stones which form the foundation on which they desire to rear the United Church.

Their pretensions, as prelatic or diocesan Bishops, are based upon the assumption that they are, as an order in the Church, distinct from and superior to Presbyters, *de jure divino*, or by express scriptural authority; and that their descent from the Apostles can be traced by a continued unbroken chain of episcopally-ordained men, and that without prelatic Bishops, there is, to make use of the language of Bishop Taylor, "no Priest, no ordination, no consecration of the sacrament; while no absolution, no rite, or sacrament can be legitimately performed in order to eternity."

There are two propositions evidently embodied in these claims:—1st, That there exists a class of office-bearers in the Church of Christ, viz., diocesan Bishops, superior, by *Divine authority*, to Presbyters or Elders, and therefore having a right to exercise jurisdiction over them; and 2dly, That the spiritual descent of these office-bearers can be traced from

* See Appendix.

the Apostles by an unbroken chain of episcopally-ordained men. The second proposition manifestly and necessarily depends upon the first; and therefore with it we shall at present exclusively deal.

Does there exist, then, by *Divine authority*, in the Church of Christ an order of office-bearers—diocesan Bishops—superior to Presbyters? This question we are prepared to meet with an unqualified negative. We unhesitatingly affirm that, whether we turn to the Scriptures, the early Fathers, or the distinguished and learned Reformers, who were instrumental in framing and setting up the Church of England, we shall not find the shadow of reliable evidence to bolster up this pretentious claim; but that, on the contrary, we shall find clearest evidence that it is an unwarrantable and groundless assumption.

First, then, what say the Scriptures on this point? "To the law and to the testimony: if they speak not according to this word, it is because there is no light in them." That Bishops and Presbyters are one and the same, under different names, is clear to demonstration, from the following among other passages:—1st, Acts xx. 17-28,—where our readers will find, by referring to the passage, that those called "Elders" by the Apostle in the 17th verse are expressly designated "Overseers," or Bishops, in the 28th verse. 2d, Titus i. 5, 7,—where those called Elders in the 5th verse are called Bishops in the 7th. 3d, 1 Peter v. 1, 2,—where the Elders addressed in the 1st verse are exhorted in the 2d to feed the flock of God, taking the oversight thereof —*episcopountes*—expressly setting forth their standing and authority as Bishops in the Church. 4th, Phil. i. 1,—where the Apostle, in addressing his epistle to the entire Church at Philippi, makes no mention whatever of a threefold order of the ministry, but of a twofold order—Bishops and Deacons—Presbyters being included in Bishops, they being, as we have already seen, one and the same under different designations.

In the five instances in which the word Bishop is used in the New Testament, it is never employed to express or shadow forth any rule or oversight over *Presbyters* of the Church, but invariably over the *flock* of Christ. That the Bishops referred to by the Apostle Paul could not be diocesan, but parochial Bishops, is evident, for instead of exercising lordship over an extensive diocese or territory, and jurisdiction over the Presbyters labouring therein, the Church at Philippi alone had several Bishops to itself, clearly showing that they were parochial Bishops, or Elders, doing the work of the ministry in the congregation, and thus feeding the flock of God, over which the Holy Ghost had made them "Bishops," or "Overseers,"* not as "lords over God's heritage," but as "ensamples to the flock."

It is thus evident that the names Bishop and Presbyter being employed in the Scriptures indifferently and interchangeably, the class of office-

---

* The literal meaning of the Greek word translated Bishop is Overseer.

bearers designated by them are one and the same. They have the same names, the same ordination, (Acts xx. 17-28; Titus i. 5, 7,) the same qualifications, and the same duties, (1 Tim. iii. 1, 2; Titus i. 5, 7.) Presbyters, moreover, are expressly mentioned as sitting along with the Apostles as members of the Council at Jerusalem; whilst no mention is made of Bishops, (Acts xv. 2, 4, 6, 22, 23.) And Presbyters only are expressly said to ordain, (1 Tim. iv. 14.)

"The Syriac translation," says Owen, "which is so very ancient, that it comes nearest in time to the original, useth not two words, one for Bishop, another for Presbyter, as our translation and the Greek, but it hath only שׁיקּישׁ; the word in Chaldee and in Syriac signifies Presbyters, (Titus i. 5, &c.) *Constitueres, Seniores in qualibet Civitate*, verse 7, *debet enim, Senior esse irreprehensibilis*. *I have left thee in Crete to ordain Elders in every city, for an Elder* (we say Bishop) *must be blameless*. So in 1 Tim. iii. 1,—*The office of a Bishop*, as we render it out of the Greek. The Syriac reads it, *the office of a Presbyter*. Instead of *Bishops* and *Deacons* in Phil. i. 1, the Syriac reads it *Presbyters* and *Deacons*. This is a strong proof that the distinction of Bishop and Presbyter was unknown when that translation was made, for it useth not so much as different names.

"If there be any distinction between a Bishop and a Presbyter, the pre-eminence must be given by the Scripture to the Presbyters; for as our Bishops say their office, distinct from Presbyters, is to rule and govern, and the office of a Presbyter is to preach and administer the sacraments. Now, the administration of the sacraments and preaching are more excellent works than ruling and governing. The Apostle saith expressly, *that they that labour in the Word and Doctrine deserve more honour than they that rule well*, (1 Tim. v. 17.) Moreover, the Apostles style themselves *Presbyters*, but never *Bishops*. *St Peter* calls himself *Presbyter*, but never calls himself a *Bishop*. And therefore it is a wonder the Pope, his pretended successor, and those that derive their canonical succession from His Holiness, should call themselves *Bishops*, unless it be by the divine disposal to show the fallibility of their foundations.

"The Papists, who therein are imitated by some of our adversaries, do say, that the names are common, but the offices are distinct. Thus *Spensæus*, a Sorbonist, objects, *Nominum quidem esse, sed non munerum confusionem.*

"The instances mentioned above do clearly evince an identity of offices. When the Apostle bids the Presbyters of *Ephesus take heed to all the flock over which the Holy Ghost hath made them Bishops*, he does not speak of the name, but the office. And it is evident that St Peter speaks of the office, when he exhorts the Presbyters to *feed the flock, and to perform the office of Bishops* among them; so that there were as many *Bishops* as there were *Presbyters* in Churches of the Apostle's planting.

"How comes it to pass, when the Apostle reckons up the several sorts of ministers, which Christ had appointed in His Church, that he makes no mention of *Superior Bishops*, if they be so necessary as some would have us believe? He mentions *Pastors* and *Teachers*. The patrons of Episcopacy will not say Bishops are meant by Teachers, their proper work being ruling; nor can they be meant by Pastors, for Presbyters are Pastors, and exhorted to *feed the flock*. Our learned writers against Popery think it a good argument to disprove the Pope's Headship, that he is not mentioned in the list of Church officers reckoned up in the *New Testament;* no more is a Bishop superior to Presbyters so much as named in those places. If any say it is omitted, because he was to succeed the Apostles, he hath the Pope ready to join with him in the same plea for his office." *

The conclusion to which the New Testament shuts us up—that Bishops and Presbyters are identical—is in perfect harmony with the judgment of the early Fathers, and of the learned Reformers, who were instrumental in laying the foundation of the Church of England.

In proceeding to examine into the evidence of the early Fathers, and of the English Reformers, it will be necessary to bear in mind the *exact state of the question*. The question is not, Is there any evidence in the writings of the early Fathers, and

---

* Owen, "Plea for Scripture Ordination," 1693. Second Edition, 1707, pp. 14, 15.

of the English Reformers, to prove the existence of diocesan Bishops in the Church (at the time they respectively wrote) by ecclesiastical authority, as a matter of mere human appointment, on the ground of expediency and Church order? But, Is there any evidence in their writings to prove that they believed in the existence of prelatic or diocesan Bishops as an order superior to Presbyters, *de jure divino*, that is by express warrant and authoritative appointment of Christ in His Word? That is the real and only question; and it is necessary that it be kept distinctly in view, because by doing so it will be seen and found that the quotations from and references to the early Fathers and Reformers by High Churchmen and Puseyites are altogether irrelevant, inasmuch as they bear upon a totally different question from that to prove which they unwarrantably adduce them. Bearing in mind, then, the exact state of the question, we affirm, without hesitation, that the judgment of the early Fathers, and of the English Reformers, in regard to the existence of diocesan Bishops, *de jure divino*, is in entire harmony with the judgment of Scripture. Two fragments have come down to us from apostolic times, the genuineness of which has been admitted both by Presbyterians and Episcopalians— viz., the First Epistle of Clemens Romanus to the Corinthians, and the Epistle of Polycarp to the Church at Philippi. Clement is generally, and on fair authority, supposed to have been the companion of the Apostle Paul, (see Phil. iv. 3), and Polycarp was the friend and disciple of the Apostle John; so that both of them held personal intercourse with the Apostles. In his Epistle to the Corinthians, Clement speaks of two orders of office-bearers only —Bishops or Presbyters, and Deacons. So evident is this, that Lord Barrington, in his "Miscellanea Sacra," says, "Bishops with St Clement are always the same with Elders or Presbyters, as any one must see if they read the epistle, or, if they can doubt of it, must be fully convinced by the notes of the learned Mr Burton upon it."* Faber admits that beyond "all possibility of misapprehension," "no more than two orders are specified by Clement, the word Bishops being used as equivalent to the word Presbyters."† "Whatever may have been the cause," says Dr Hawkins, in his discourse on the Apostolical Succession, as also in his Bampton Lectures, "the Church of Corinth appears, as I conceive from the Epistle of Clement, not to have had its Bishop, as well as its Presbyters and Deacons." In his epistle, Clement speaks of the "flock of Christ with the Presbyters, who are set over it," and of the happiness of those "Presbyters" who had finished "their EPISCOPACY," before the dissensions arose in the Church, on account of which he rebuked them, thus clearly proving that Presbyters and Bishops were one and the same—Episcopacy, or the office of being overseers over the flock, being common to both. Bishop Croft's testimony, as

* Vol. ii., p. 154. Ed. 1770.
† The Ancient Vallenses, p. 558.

given in his "True State of the Primitive Church," is clear and decided. "In this epistle," says Bishop Croft, "Clement particularly sets forth the constitution of the Church by the Apostles, and what ministers they ordained in the Church—to wit, Bishops and Deacons; he names no others, which seems to me as full an evidence as can be that there were no other orders in the Church in those days but those two; and yet we are sure that there were then Presbyters in the Church, for St Peter calls them Presbyters to whom he wrote his epistle; so that if there were but two orders—to wit, Bishops and Deacons—Presbyters must be one and the same with Bishops or with Deacons; not with Deacons, therefore one and the same with Bishops —one order called by two names promiscuously in Scripture, as hath been showed before."*

We come now to the testimony of Polycarp, the disciple of the Apostle John, and called by Irenæus "the blessed and apostolic Presbyter." In his epistle to "the Church of God which is at Philippi," he makes mention only of Presbyters and Deacons, and no mention whatever of Bishops, or of any order superior to Presbyters. When Paul addressed his epistle to the Church at Philippi, there existed only two orders of office-bearers in that Church— "Bishops and Deacons;" and now seventy years after the death of the Apostles, when Polycarp addresses his epistle to the same Church, we find two orders only still existing. The threefold order

* Scott's Col. of Tr., vol. vii., p. 298, quoted by Smyth.

of the ministry, in the prelatic sense, is nowhere to be found. We say in the prelatic sense, for in the Presbyterian Church there is, in the twofold order of office-bearers, a threefold distinction, (grounded upon 1 Tim. v. 17, and Acts iv. 1-7)—viz., the Elders or Presbyters, "that rule;" the Presbyters, "who labour in word and doctrine;" and the Deacons, who "serve tables," attending to the financial and secular affairs of the Church. "So far, then," says the late lamented Principal Cunningham, "as concerns the *only* two apostolic men, of whom it is generally admitted that we have their remains genuine and uncorrupted, it is evident that their testimony upon this point entirely concurs with Scripture—that they furnish no evidence whatever of the existence of Prelacy, and that their testimony runs clearly and decidedly in favour of Presbyterial government; and if so, then this is a blow struck at the root or foundation of the whole alleged prelatic testimony from antiquity. It cuts off the first and most important link in the chain, and leaves a gap between the Apostles and any subsequent Prelacy which cannot be filled up."

We shall now examine the alleged testimony of Ignatius—the sheet-anchor of Episcopalians—and the testimony of the great English Reformers.

I. The testimony of Ignatius, who was contemporary with Polycarp. Of the fifteen epistles at one time ascribed to him, eight have long ago been set aside as forgeries. Archbishop Usher, who devoted not a little time and labour to an examination of these epistles, and who published a Latin translation of seven of them, admits that of the twelve epistles rejected by Salmatius, and other learned divines, he has "certain proof that six of them are counterfeits, and that the remaining six are corrupted by interpolations in very many places." Of the six or seven epistles whose genuineness Bishop Pearson and others have laboured hard to establish, four have been, on most sufficient grounds, struck off the list by Dr Cureton, who has satisfactorily shown that only the three letters contained in the Syriac MS. are entitled to be considered as, in any respect, genuine; and we may add that, as regards these three, there is no reason to conclude that they are free from interpolations. Dr Goode, Dean of Ripon,* than whom no divine of the Church of England is more conversant with patristic literature, affirms that no works have been more extensively mutilated and corrupted than those of the Fathers, so much so that "above one hundred and eighty treatises, professing to be written by authors of the first six centuries, are repudiated by the more learned of the Romanists themselves as most of them rank forgeries, and the others as not written by those whose names they bear. But, what is worse, we have also to guard against the corruptions introduced into the *genuine works* of the Fathers, an evil which has been growing *since the very earliest times.*" And, then, quoting from Anastasius Sinaita, he goes on to say, " There was a certain Augustan prefect,

* Since the above was written, Dr Goode has died.

(at Alexandria,) a follower of Severus, who for a long time had fourteen amanuenses of like mind with himself, to sit down at his command and falsify the books containing the doctrines of the Fathers, and especially those of the holy Cyril."—Goode's *Rule of Faith*, vol. i., pp. 194–6.

Three epistles, then, only remain, and along with the spurious ones disappear the "mass of stuff about Bishops, Presbyters, and Deacons, with which the former editions were crammed." Of the one and only passage which is left, and which occurs in the Epistle to Polycarp, c. 6, Dr Cunningham justly affirms that "there is certainly nothing in the least resembling it, either in language or in spirit, in the New Testament, or in Clement and Polycarp, and it may fairly be regarded as an interpolation."

Dr Killen, in his "History of the Early Church," sets aside the Ignatian Epistles, one and all, as entirely spurious; and we believe that Episcopalians will have considerable difficulty in meeting the arguments on which he grounds his judgment regarding them.

But even supposing the Epistles of Ignatius to be genuine, the language contained in them regarding Presbyters is such as to preclude the possibility of any lordship over them by Bishops, *de jure divino*. In his Epistle to the Smyrnians he says, "See that ye follow the *Presbyters as Apostles*." In his Epistle to the Magnesians he says, "The Presbyters preside in the place of the Council of the Apostles." In his Epistle to the Trallians he says, "Be ye subject to your Presbyters as to the Apostles of Jesus Christ, our hope." " Let all reverence the Presbyters as the Sanhedrim of God, and College of Apostles." If the epistles, therefore, bring before us a class of office-bearers in the Church, exercising lordship over " Presbyters who preside in the place of the Council of the Apostles," and who constitute " the Sanhedrim of God and College of the Apostles," they necessarily shut us up to the conclusion that, if genuine to any extent, they are self-contradictory, have been interpolated, and are therefore not reliable. Their utter worthlessness, for High Church purposes, cannot be better expressed than in the deliverance come to regarding them by one of the greatest departed ornaments of the Church of England, the learned Bishop Stillingfleet. " In all those thirty-five testimonies," says Stillingfleet, in his Irenicum, " produced out of Ignatius's Epistles for Episcopacy, I can meet with but one which is brought to prove the least resemblance of an *Institution of Christ for Episcopacy;* and if I be not much deceived, the sense of that place is clearly mistaken too." *

The learned historian, Bingham, is a high authority with Episcopalians, and he justly says of Jerome, the most learned of the Latin Fathers—" St Jerome will be allowed to speak the sense of the ancients." We conclude, therefore, the evidence from the early Fathers, with that of Jerome, of whom Augustine declared that a more learned man never lived. What then says Jerome in regard to the

* Irenicum, p. 309, Ed. 1662.

identity of Presbyters and Bishops? He says "Presbyters and Bishops were FORMERLY THE SAME. And before the devil incited men to make divisions in religion, and one was led to say, 'I am of Paul, and I of Apollos,' churches were governed by the common Council of Presbyters." And, after referring to the Epistle to the Philippians, the Acts of the Apostles, and the First Epistle of Peter, he says, "These passages we have brought forward to show that, with the ancients, *Presbyters were the same as Bishops.* But that the roots of dissension might be plucked up, a *usage gradually* took place that the chief care should devolve upon one. Therefore, as the Presbyters know that it is by the custom of the Church that they are to be subject to him who is placed over them, so let the Bishops know that they are above Presbyters rather by *custom than by Divine appointment,* and that the Church ought to be ruled in common," (Note on Titus i.) Nor did Jerome stand alone in holding this opinion. No. "I believe," says Stillingfleet, in his Irenicum, "upon the strictest inquiry, Medina's judgment will prove true, that Hieron, Austin, Ambrose, Sedulius, Primasius, Chrysostom, Theodoret, and Theophylact, were all of Aerius's judgment as to the *identity* of both *name* and *order* of Bishops and Presbyters in the Primitive Church."* We have thus the testimony of the Apostolic Fathers, Clement and Polycarp, that, in their day, there were only two distinct orders of office-bearers in the Church—viz., Presbyters or

---

* Irenicum, p. 276.

Bishops and Deacons; and we have also the express testimony of Jerome, who flourished in the fourth century, and who was the most learned of the Latin Fathers, that Bishops and Presbyters were originally one and the same; but that a usage gradually took place, that the chief care should devolve upon one; and, therefore, he would have the Bishops remember that they are above Presbyters, not "by divine appointment," but "by custom," and, therefore, "that the Church ought to be ruled in common."

II. So much, then, for the testimony of the early Fathers. Let us now endeavour to ascertain what testimony the learned Reforming Fathers of the Church of England have left in regard to this point. "I boldly assert," says Wickliffe, "that in the Primitive Church, or in the time of Paul, two orders of the clergy were sufficient—that is, a priest and a deacon. In like manner I affirm, that in the time of Paul, the Presbyter and Bishop were names of the *same office*. This appears from the third chapter of the First Epistle to Timothy, and in the first chapter of the Epistle to Titus. And the same is testified by that profound theologian, Jerome."* Now in this judgment, the framers of the formularies and authoritative standards of the Church of England unqualifiedly concur. In 1537, a convocation of Archbishops, Bishops, and learned Divines was held, at which Cromwell, the King's Vicar-General, was present, as his Majesty's representative. A document was drawn up by them,

* "Life of Wickliffe," (Vaughan's), vol. i"., p. 275. Ed. 1831.

and in that document, to quote the words of Bishop Burnet regarding it. Bishops and Priests are spoken of as *one and the same office.* The document itself is entitled the "Institution of a Christian Man." It is also known as the "Bishop's Book." In that document we have "A Declaration made of the Functions and Divine Institution of Bishops and Priests."

The following extracts on "The Functions and Divine Institution of Bishops and Priests," will show clearly the views of its framers in regard to the office of the ministry :—

"As touching the Sacraments of the *Holy Orders*, we will that all Bishops and Preachers shall instruct and teach our people committed by us unto their spiritual charge—

"First, How that Christ and His Apostles did institute, and ordained, in the New Testament, certain ministers, or officers, which should have spiritual power, authority, and commission, under Christ, to preach, &c., and to order and consecrate others, in the same room, order, and office, whereunto they be called and admitted themselves; and, finally, to feed Christ's people, like good pastors and rectors," &c.

"Item, That this office, this ministration, this power and authority, is no tyrannical power, having no certain laws or limits within the which it ought to be contained; nor yet none absolute power; but it is a moderate power, subject, determined, and restrained unto those certain limits and ends for the which the same was appointed by God's ordinance."

"Item, That this office, this power and authority was committed, and given by Christ and His apostles, unto certain persons only, that is to say, unto Priests, or Bishops, whom they did elect, call, and admit thereunto by their prayer and imposition of their hands."

And then, after stating that "albeit the Holy Fathers of the Church did also institute certain inferior orders, or degrees," it concludes with this clear and decided judgment: "YET THE TRUTH IS, THAT IN THE NEW TESTAMENT *there is no mention made of any degrees or distinctions in orders, but only of Deacons or Ministers, and of Priests or Bishops.*"

In this authoritative document of the Church of England, signed by Thomas (Lord) Cromwell, (the King's Vicar-General), by Cranmer, Archbishop of Canterbury, by the Archbishop of York, by the Bishops of London, Durham, Lincoln, Bath, Ely, Bangor, Salisbury, Hereford, Worcester, Rochester, and Chichester, along with upwards of twenty of the most eminent "Doctors of Laws, and Doctors of Divinity," in England,—in this document in which the Church of England formally lays down and declares "the *functions* and *divine institution* of Bishops and Priests"—that is, Presbyters, it is expressly taught and affirmed, that, by the New Testament, Bishops and Presbyters are one and the same order and office, and that, by commission under Christ, the "spiritual power and authority" of Bishops and Presbyters "to preach, &c.; and to order and consecrate others in the same room, order, and office whereunto they be called and admitted themselves," are equal, being one and the same.

In 1543, "The King's Book," otherwise called, "The Necessary Erudition of a Christian Man," was published by *royal authority*. Fuller and Burnet inform us, that the able and learned divines who drew it up, were authoritatively appointed for the purpose.

It was read and approved of by the Lords spiritual and temporal, and the Lower House of Parliament; and Dr Laurence, in his Bampton Lecture, informs us, that, "before its publication, it was approved of by the Convocation then sitting, in which it was examined in parts, as appears evident from the minutes of that Assembly, in Wilkins's *Concilia Magnæ Brittaniæ*, v. 3, p. 868." Now, this Book, drawn up by a Committee of Bishops and Divines, appointed by the Crown for the purpose, examined and approved of by the Convocation then sitting, read and approved by both Houses of Parliament, and constituting, therefore, one of the highest legal standard authorities of the Church of England, lays down the doctrine, that Presbyters and Bishops are, by God's law, one and the same; that "*of two orders only*, that is to say, Priests and Deacons, Scripture maketh express mention;" that "Christ sets them *all*, (viz., ministers), indifferently,

AND IN LIKE POWER, DIGNITY, and AUTHORITY; and that all lawful authority and powers of one Bishop over another were to be given to them by the consent or ordinance, *and positive laws of men only*, AND NOT BY ANY ORDINANCE OF GOD IN HOLY SCRIPTURE."

We thus see, that whether we appeal to the Word of God, the early Fathers, or the founders of the Church of England, " Presbyters and Bishops are one and the same office ;" that, originally, there was no difference between them; and that the superiority which Bishops obtained over Presbyters after the Apostolic period, in the third or fourth centuries, as well as in the Church of England, was not by a divine ordinance, but by mere human appointment, on grounds of expediency and Church order; and that " the threefold order of the ministry," of which the Roman Catholic, Greek, and Anglican Churches boast as their exclusive heritage and peculiar possession, *is not a doctrine of the Word of God, but an invention of man.*

To the learned Reformers of the Church of England, might be added a catalogue of names, the most celebrated in divinity, church history, and literature of which the world has ever heard. Melancthon, Calvin, Beza, Vitringa, Erasmus, Claude, Grotius, Bochart, M. Flacius Illyricus, Blondell, Milton, Zanchius, &c., &c., all held that the superiority of Bishops to Presbyters is not by divine appointment, but by mere ecclesiastical arrangement; while the most eminent modern biblical critics in our own day, as Alford, Ellicot, Bloomfield, &c., have come to the same conclusion as Whitaker, Jewell, Reynolds, Cranmer, Field, Usher, Mosheim, Burnet, Stillingfleet, Whitby, Scott, and Neander—himself a host—that, in the New Testament—in the Acts of the Apostles, the 1st Epistle to Timothy, and the Epistle to Titus— Bishops and Presbyters are one and the same, the terms being "applied *indifferently to the same person.*"

"Without entering," says Bishop Ellicot, "into any description of the origin of Episcopacy generally, it seems proper to remark that we must fairly acknowledge with Jerome, that in the pastoral epistles, the terms Episcopos and Presbyteros are applied indifferently to the same person." In commenting on Paul's address to the Elders at Ephesus, Dean Alford says, "The English version has hardly done fairly in this case with the sacred text, in rendering Episcopous, ver. 28, 'overseers,' whereas it ought there, as in all other places, to have been 'Bishops,' that the fact of Elders—or Presbyters—and Bishops having been *originally and apostolically synonymous*, might be apparent to the ordinary English reader, which now it is not."

If then, the doctrine of the superiority of diocesan Bishops to Presbyters, by express appointment of the Word of God, was unknown in the Church of England in the days of the Reformers who drew up her Articles and Formularies, when, it may be asked, was the doctrine first taught within her pale? We believe it will be found that it was not till about half a century after the "Declaration of the Functions and Divine Institution of Bishops and Priests," had been emitted; and then, merely by an individual—Dr Bancroft.

In a sermon preached at Paul's Cross, on the 9th of February, 1588, referring to the case of Aerius, Dr Bancroft evidently intended that his hearers should draw the conclusion, that to teach that there was no difference, by divine right, between a Bishop and a Presbyter, was heresy. This doctrine fell with startling effect upon the ears of those who heard it. It was strange doctrine to them; and it occasioned so much surprise, as being altogether different from the teaching of the Reformers down to that time, that Sir Francis Knollis wrote to Dr Reynolds, who was reputed to be the most learned divine in the Church of England at that period, to ask his opinion regarding it. The doctor wrote him in reply, that the doctrine laid down by Bancroft was untenable; refers him to the controversy which Bishop Jewell had with the Jesuit Harding upon the same point, and to the bishop's triumphant demolition of the Jesuit's assertions, citing Chrysostom, Austin, Hierome, Ambrose, &c., &c., to show that they all held and maintained views entirely opposed to those of Harding, which were the same as Bancroft's. And after citing many eminent authorities, in addition to those brought forward by Jewell, Dr Reynolds concludes by affirming that, for five hundred years previous, all who had been actively in favour of reforming the Church, have been of opinion "that all pastors, whether called Bishops or Presbyters, have, according to the Word of God, like power and authority."

Down to this time, the Reformers in England, Scotland, and on the Continent were agreed on all essential points; but this sermon threatened to dig a gulf between them; and the novel and unscriptural character of Dr Bancroft's views were so conclusively shown, that he himself afterwards modified them, and acknowledged the validity of the orders of the foreign churches in which Episcopacy had no place.

We have thus dwelt upon the apostolic identity of Bishops and Presbyters, in order to make it clear to our readers, that the threefold order of the ministry, in the prelatic sense of diocesan Bishops, Presbyters, and Deacons, has no place in the Word of God, had no place in the Primitive Church in the days of the Apostolic Fathers, and had a place given to it in the Church of England, not on any alleged ground of *divine right*, but solely on grounds of expediency and Church order, and in consequence of the High Church tendencies and predilections of Henry and Elizabeth. The only Bishops of which the New Testament knows anything, are Presbyters or Elders—Bishops parochial, not diocesan—in other words, Bishops, not of a diocese, but of a congregation, "over which the Holy Ghost hath made them 'overseers,' to feed the Church of God which He hath purchased with His own blood;" "taking the oversight (*episcopountes*) thereof, not for filthy lucre, but of a ready mind ; neither as being lords over God's heritage, but being ensamples to the flock."

It is right that, in these days of priestly pretensions, when Episcopacy is lifting up its head loftily among us, our Presbyterian readers should know that our doctrine in regard to the government of the Church is "founded on the Word of God, and agreeable thereto ;" that it is Episcopalians, not we, who require to give a reason for their Church polity; that Scripture, the early fathers, and the concurrent testimony of the greatest Protestant divines of the Reformation period throughout the world, are as clearly in our favour, as they are opposed to the extravagant and unwarrantable pretensions of Scotch Episcopacy and English Tractarianism.

The appointment of congregational Bishops or overseers, by the Holy Ghost, *over the flock of Christ*, we can prove by express reference to the Word of God. The entire bench of Bishops might safely be challenged to cite one passage from the same divine source—the only infallible rule of doctrine and of government—to prove the appointment of diocesan Bishops, by the Holy Ghost, as overseers *over the ministers of Christ*. Such evidence never has been produced, and never will. It does not exist, and therefore cannot be found.

That the doctrine of Jerome and of the English Reformers was also the doctrine of the early English Church, is evident from the Canons of Elfric to Bishop Wulfin, of date 957 ; also from Archbishop Peckham's Constitutions, of date 1281. Both enumerate the seven orders appointed in the Church as follows :—1. The Ostiary. 2. The Lector. 3. The Exorcist. 4. The Acolyth. 5. The Sub-deacon. 6. The Deacon. 7. The Presbyter.

The order of Bishop is not specified, being included in, and identical with, that of Presbyter. "There is no more difference," says Elfric, "between the Mass-Presbyter and the Bishop, but that the Bishop is appointed to ordain, to hallow Churches, and to see to the execution of the laws of God, which, if every Presbyter should do it, would be committed to too many. Both, indeed, are one and the same order, although the part of the Bishop is the more honourable.*

That the celebrated Anselm, Archbishop of Canterbury, was of the same opinion, is clear from his Commentary on the first chapter of Titus, and the first chapter of the Epistle to the Philippians.

As regards the early Scottish Church, it has been clearly shown by writers from the earliest times down to authors of our own time, as Dr M'Lauchlan and Hill Burton, that *Diocesan Episcopacy* was unknown in it, and the same may be said of the early Irish Church. Bede admits that in Iona the Bishops were subjected to the Presbyter Abbot, who was at the head of the institution.† Hill Burton

---

* Johnston's Canons and Constitutions of the Church of England since *the Conquest,* and before the Reformation. Ed. 1720. Canones, &c., a Laur. Howell, pp. 66, 67. Ed. 1708.

† Habere solet ipsa insula rectorem semper Abbatem Presbyterum, Cujus Juri et omnis Provincia, et ipsi etiam Episcopi,

clearly shows that the Bishops of the early Irish Church were parochial or congregational, not diocesan Bishops :—

"The Bishops consecrated by St Patrick alone were counted by hundreds. One of the more moderate estimates makes them three hundred and sixty-five—just one for every day in the year. Whether or not we believe all that is said about their multitudinousness, *it is beyond doubt that the early Bishops were so numerous, that the most resolute champions of diocesan Episcopacy cannot find for them provinces with corporations of Presbyters over whom they held diocesan rule.*"—(Hill Burton, vol. i., p. 269.) He adds that, when the Papacy extended its influence to Ireland, these Bishops were converted into rural deans.

It is evident that St Patrick's Bishops were similar to the *Chorepiscopi*, or rural Bishops of the Primitive Church, whose Bishopric was but a single congregation, as has been ably shown by Lord King in his "Inquiry into the Constitution, Discipline, Unity, and Worship of the Primitive Church."

"It is no marvel," says Lord King, (Ed. 1713, p. 40), "that we find Bishops not only in cities, but *in country villages*, there being a Bishop constituted wherever there were believers enough to form a competent congregation : For, says *Clemens Ro-*

ordine inusitato debeant esse subjecti, juxta Exemplum Primi Doctoris illius, qui non Episcopus, sed Presbyter extitit et Monachus. Bed. Hist. iii. 4.

manus, the Apostles going forth, and preaching both in *country* and city, constituted *Bishops and Deacons* there. Much to which purpose Cyprian says, *Per omnes provincias, et per urbes singulas ordinati sunt Episcopi.* Bishops were ordained throughout all provinces and cities. Hence, in the Encyclical Epistle of the Synod of Antioch, it is said that *Paulus* Samosatenus had many flatterers amongst the adjacent city and *country Bishops;* of this sort of *country Bishops* was *Zoticus, Bishop of the village* of Comane. And we may reasonably believe that many of those bishops who in the year 258 were assembled at *Carthage* to the number of fourscore and seven, had no other than obscure villages for their seats, since we find not the least notice of them in *Ptolemy* or any of the old geographers."

To the testimonies already cited from Scripture, the apostolic Fathers, and the Reformers of the Church of England, in proof of the scriptural identity of Bishops and Presbyters, might be added the testimony of the most distinguished among the Schoolmen, and the Canonists, and also that of Pope Urban II. The Master of the Sentences saith, "*Apud veteres iidem Episcopi et Presbyteri fuerunt.*" He adds, "*Excellenter Canones duos tantum sacros ordines Appellari censent, Diaconatus,* &c., *et Presbyteratus, quia hos solos primitiva Ecclesia legitur habuisse et de his solis præceptum Apostoli habemus,*" (Lib. iv., dist. 24.) Bonaventure, in 4 sent. dist. 24, Q. 1, A. 1, *Episcopatus deficit ab ordine,* &c., *includit necessario ordinem perfectissimum,* &c.,

sacerdotium. With whom agree Durand, Dominic, Aureolus, &c., who all comment upon *Lombard's* text.—See Aquinas's Supplem., quæst. 37, art. 2. Gratian's judgment is thus expressed:—" *Sacros ordines dicimus Diaconatum et Presbyteratum, hos quidem solos Ecclesia primitiva habuisse dicitur.*" *Johannes Senneca*, in his Gloss on the Canon Law, affirms that Bishops and Presbyters in the Primitive Church, both as respects their names and offices, were identical; but that in the age succeeding that of the Primitive Church, the names and the offices began to be distinguished. *Nomina erant communia, et officium erat commune, sed in secunda primitiva* cæperunt distingui, et *nomina, et officia,* (quoted by Owen, in his *Plea for Scripture Ordination*;) who also shows that in the Council of *Aix la Chapelle*, and the Council of *Hispalis*, the identity of Bishops and Presbyters was acknowledged; while in the Councils of *Constance* and *Basil*, after long debate, it was concluded that Presbyters should have decisive suffrages in councils, as well as Bishops, because, by the law of God, *Bishops were no more than Presbyters*, and it is expressly given them (Acts. xv. 23.)—*Owen's Plea*, pp. 108–9.

CHAPTER II.

THE RULING ELDER—SUBORDINATION OF CHURCH COURTS.

In the preceding chapter it is stated that in the Presbyterian Church, there is, in the twofold order of office-bearers, a threefold distinction—viz., the Elders or Presbyters "that rule," the Presbyters, "who labour in the word and doctrine," and the Deacons, who "serve tables," attending to the financial and secular affairs of the Church.

That the Presbyters were divided into two classes—those who only ruled, and those who not only ruled, but also laboured in the word and doctrine—is evident from Rom. xii. 6, 7, 8, where the Ruler is distinguished from the Teacher and Exhorter; from 2 Cor. xii. 28, where "governments," or those invested with the power of ruling, are distinguished from the Prophets and Teachers; and from 1 Tim. v. 17, where the Ruling Elder is expressly distinguished from the Elders who not only rule, but also labour in the word and doctrine.

In his "Assertion of the Government of the Church of Scotland," Gillespie shows, at great length, that the office of Ruling Elder has existed in the Church from Apostolic times, and cites numerous authorities in proof from the early Fathers, and the most eminent Protestant Divines. (See Part I., chaps. vii. to xiii.)

In the "Form of Presbyterial Church Government, agreed upon by the Assembly of Divines at Westminster, with the assistance of Commissioners from the Church of Scotland," it is affirmed that it is lawful and agreeable to the Word of God that the Church be governed by several sorts of Assemblies, which are "congregational," (kirk sessions) "classical," (Presbyteries) "and synodical," and also "that there be a subordination of congregational, classical, provincial, and national assemblies, for the government of the Church," (see Matt. xviii. 15–20; 1 Cor. v. 4, compared with 2 Cor. ii. 6; Acts xiii. 1, in connection with Acts xv. 1–31), in which passages we have clear warrant for congregational, Presbyterial, and Synodical or General Assemblies, for the government of the Church, hearing and deciding causes, admonishing, censuring, excommunicating impenitent scandalous offenders, and restoring penitents.

In the 15th chapter of the Acts of the Apostles we have an account of a difficulty which arose in the Church at Antioch. After no small dissension and disputation in the Court, or congregational assembly at Antioch, it was "determined that Paul and Barnabas, and certain other of them," should go up to Jerusalem to submit the case to a General Assembly there. The Assembly met. The case was fully heard; and, after reasoning, a judgment was come to and recorded, and an extract minute was sent to the Church at Antioch, which had the effect of satisfactorily disposing of the question.

The case was one of false doctrine arising in the Church, in consequence of which the members of the Church were troubled, and their souls in danger of being subverted; and the authoritative juridical acts of the Council, corresponded to the "threefold power of jurisdiction," competent to Church Courts, viz., the *dogmatic,* the *diatactic,* and the *critic*—δογματικὴ, διατακτικη, κριτικη.

"1. *Against the heresie broached*—viz., that they must be circumcised, and keep the ceremonial law of Moses, or else they could not be saved (Acts xv. 2.) The Synod put forth a *dogmatique power*, in confutation of the heresie, and clear vindication of the truth, about the great point of *justification by faith* without the works of the law, (Acts xv. 7–23.)

"2. Against the *schism*, occasioned by the doctrine of the false Teachers that troubled the Church, (Acts xv. 1, 2), the Synod put forth a *critick*, or *censuring power*, stigmatising the false Teachers with the infamous brands of *troubling the Church with words, subverting of souls,* and (tacitly, as some conceive from that expression, *Unto whom we gave no such commandment,* v. 24) of belying the Apostles and Elders of Jerusalem, as if they had sent them abroad to preach this doctrine.

" 3. Against the *scandal* of the weak Jews, and their heart-estrangement from the Gentiles, who neglected their ceremonial observances; as also against the *scandal* of the Gentiles, who were much troubled and offended at the urging of circumcision, and the keeping of the law as necessary to salvation, (ver. 1, 2, 19, 24), the Synod put forth a *diatactick ordering* or *regulating power*, framing practical rules or constitutions, for the healing of the scandal, and for prevention of the spreading of it, commanding the brethren of the several Churches to abstain from divers things that might any way occasion the same."*

* *Jus Divinum Regiminis Ecclesiastici.* By Sundry Ministers of Christ within the City of London. Edition 1654, pp. 246–47.

CHAPTER III.

ARGUMENT FROM THE CASES OF TIMOTHY, TITUS, AND THE ANGELS OF THE SEVEN CHURCHES.

It has been asserted by Prelatists, in support of their system of Church government, that Timothy and Titus were Bishops in the prelatic sense,—the one of Ephesus, and the other of Crete. The evidence on which this assertion is founded is 1 Tim. i. 3: "As I besought thee to abide still at Ephesus, when I went into Macedonia, that thou mightest charge some that they teach no other doctrine." And Titus i. 5, "For this cause left I thee in Crete, that thou shouldest set in order the things that are wanting, and ordain elders in every city, as I had appointed thee."

At the period referred to in the foregoing passages, in which Paul delivers these instructions to Timothy and Titus, the foundations of the New Testament Church were being laid. The builders had to do, not with an *ecclesia constituta*—a Church formally settled and put in order—but with an *ecclesia con-*

stituenda—a Church in course of being formed; and, therefore, extraordinary officers were needed to meet the exigencies of an extraordinary time. Just as at the Reformation in Scotland, in 1560, when *superintendents* were appointed over *dioceses* or *provinces*, who received instructions to set in order the things which were wanting, to plant Churches, and ordain Elders over them, but who, nevertheless, were not considered to belong to an order different from that of the other Presbyters; but, in their Presbyteries and Assemblies, were on a footing of perfect equality, ordinary ministers being frequently elected as Moderators of the General Assembly, when the superintendents were present simply as members. All Christian missionaries, in gathering out and building up Churches in heathen lands, have to perform the same duties as fell to Timothy and Titus to discharge, viz., "to set in order the things that are wanting," to plant Churches, and ordain Elders over them; but the performance of these duties does not, in any way whatever, exalt them to an order in the ministry of a higher nature, *jure divino*, than that of the Presbyterate.

Although Timothy received miraculous gifts by the imposition of Paul's hands (for the Apostles had power to confer such gifts), yet *his ordination was by "the laying on of the hands of the Presbytery."*

As for Titus, so far from being a Bishop, in the prelatic sense of the term, the Apostle, when giving him instructions as to the way and manner in which he was to perform his duties in Crete, does so in language which clearly demonstrates that Bishops and Presbyters are one and the same order of ecclesiastical office-bearers, making use of the terms interchangeably, thus plainly teaching Titus that, in ordaining *Elders*, he was ordaining *Bishops*, inasmuch as they were identical.

Dr Whitby, one of the ablest Episcopal divines, confesses, "that, in regard to the great controversy whether Timothy and Titus were indeed Bishops, the one of Ephesus and the other of Crete, he can find nothing of that matter in any writer *of the three first centuries*, nor any intimation that they bore that name." He also admits that "there is no satisfactory evidence of Timothy having resided longer at Ephesus than was necessary to execute a special and temporary mission to that Church."* While another able defender of Episcopacy, the erudite Dodwell, affirms that they were itinerating, and not resident officers, who aided the Apostles in founding and settling Churches. And this is in perfect harmony with the description given by Eusebius of the special duties of an evangelist, when he says that he was appointed to "lay the foundations of the faith in barbarous nations, to constitute them pastors, and having committed to them the cultivating of those new plantations, to pass on to other countries and nations."

It is hardly necessary to inform the reader that the postscript to the Second Epistle to Timothy and the postscript to the Epistle to Titus, form no part

* Commentary on Titus, preface.

of the Holy Scriptures; that they are mere interpolations added several centuries after the epistles were written; that in several of the oldest versions of the original Scriptures — including the *Codex Vaticanus*, published at Rome, under the editorial care of Cardinal Mai—these postscripts are not to be found; and that, in short, they possess no value or authority whatever.

Not a little has been attempted to be made in support of the scriptural authority of diocesan Bishops, from the epistles to the seven Churches of Asia. These epistles are addressed to the angels of the Churches; and these angels, it is contended, must have been Bishops. Congregational, or in other words, parochial or scriptural Bishops they may have been, but not a shadow of evidence can be brought forward to warrant their being transformed into prelatic Bishops. From the scope and language of the epistles, the expression would seem to be employed in a collective sense, including the entire body of the ministry, represented by their Moderator or President; but whether in a collective or in a singular sense, there is nothing whatever in the language employed that makes it more suitable to Bishops than to Presbyters,—to a diocesan Bishop, than to the Moderator of a Kirk Session or Presbytery.

The Christian Church was formed, not after the model of the Jewish temple, but of the Jewish synagogue. This is unanswerably shown by Grotius, Lightfoot, Vitringa, Stillingfleet, Neander, Rosenmüller, &c.

"St John, a Jew, calls the ministers of particular or parochial Churches *the angels of the Churches*, in the style of the Jewish Church, who called the public minister of every synagogue שליח׳ציבור—Sheliach Tsibbor—*the Angel of the Church*. They called him also or *Bishop*, or superintendent, *of the congregation*. Every synagogue, or congregation, had its *Bishop*, or *Angel, of the Church*. Now, the service and worship of the Temple being abolished as being ceremonial, God transplanted the worship and public adoration used in the synagogues, which was moral, into the Christian Church, to wit, the public ministry, public prayers, reading God's Word, and preaching, &c. Hence the names of the ministers of the gospel were the very same, *the Angel of the Church* and the *Bishop*, which belonged to the ministers in the synagogue. We love Bishops so well, that we could wish we had as many *Bishops* as there are parishes in England, as the Jewish synagogues had to which St John alludes, when he calls them *Angels of the Churches*."—*Owen's Plea*, p. 37.

"If many things," says Stillingfleet, "in the epistles be directed to the Angel, but yet so as to concern the whole body, then of necessity the Angel must be taken as representative of the body, either of the whole Church, or which is far more probable, of the *Concessus*, or order of Presbyters of that Church."—*Irenicum*, p. 290.

The Apostle John, through whom the messages to the Churches were delivered, frequently makes use of the expression *Presbyter*, or *Elder*, both in the Apocalypse and in his epistles, but never of *Bishop;* and hints, as has been well said, at no primacy, except the attempted primacy of *Diotrephes*, which he indignantly denounces and refers to as a beacon to warn us of what is to be avoided, not as an example to be imitated.

CHAPTER IV.

ON THE RIGHTS AND STANDING OF PRESBYTERS IN CONFERRING ORDINATION.

The Doctrine of the Church of England—Of the Scotch Episcopal Church—Archbishops Sancroft, Wake, Secker, Usher, Potter, Howley—Bishops Morton, Cosin, Wordsworth, &c.

"A Bishop at his first erection was nothing else but *Primus Presbyter*, or Episcopus Praeses (as a Moderator in a Church Assembly, or a Speaker in a Parliament,) that governed *communi concilio Presbyterorum*, and had neither power of ordination, nor of jurisdiction, but in common with his Presbyters. Ambrose, upon 1 Tim. iii., saith, 'That there is *one and the same ordination*[*] *of a Bishop and a Presbyter;* for both of them are Priests, but the Bishop is the first.' Even according to the judgment of antiquity, Presbyters have an intrinsical power and authority to ordain Ministers, and when this power was restrained, and inhibited, it was not *propter legis necessitatem*, but only *propter honorem sacerdotii;* it was not from the canon of the Scriptures, but from some canons of the Church."—*The Divine Right of the Ministry of England*, 1654.

HAVING established the identity of Bishops and Presbyters from Scripture, the Apostolic Fathers,

[*] *Episcopi et Presbyteri una est ordinatio; uterq. enim sacerdos est, sed episcopus primus.*

and the Founders of the Church of England, we have now to point out the difference between the Church of England and the Scotch Episcopal Church, respecting the validity of ordination by Presbyters, and the rights and standing of Presbyters in conferring ordination. In the Church of England Presbyters are ordained by the Bishop, along with the Presbyters, the presence of at least three Presbyters being necessary,—the right of Presbyters to take part in that solemn act being expressly recognised and provided for. In the Scotch Episcopal Church the Bishop *alone* ordains, and the Presbyters are entirely excluded from taking any part whatever.* In the first canon of the Scotch Episcopal Church it is expressly declared, that "the right of consecration and ordination belongs to the order of Bishops only;" while in the Church of England it is ordered that the Bishop, with the Presbyters present, shall lay their hands severally upon the head of every one that receiveth the order of the Presbyterate, the Bishop saying, "Receive the Holy Ghost for the office and work of a Priest"—that is, Presbyter—"in the Church of God, now committed unto thee by the imposition of OUR hands,"—the right and competency of the Presbyters to take part in the act of conferring ordination being acknowledged as distinctly as that of the Bishop. We have already shown that, although the three orders of Bishops, Presbyters,

* In direct antagonism to Canons ii. and xx. of the Council of Carthage.

and Deacons, are specified in the formularies of the Church of England, the distinction between Bishop and Presbyter was not held by the Fathers of that Church to be by Divine right, but merely on grounds of expediency and ecclesiastical arrangements; and, accordingly, we find that, in the original book for ordaining Presbyters and Bishops, which was drawn up in the reign of Edward VI., there is no difference whatever in the words of the service for ordaining a Bishop to distinguish his office from that of a Presbyter. For upwards of a hundred years, in the Church of England, the ordination service for Bishops and Presbyters was one and the same,—the same portions of Scripture were referred to as the ground upon which the service was based; thus clearly proving that, in the opinion of the early Reformers of the Church of England, there was no difference between the order of Bishop and Presbyter, by *Divine institution*, but simply by ecclesiastical arrangement. The change in the ordination service was made in the reign of Charles II., in 1662, by the Bishops who revised the service, at a time when High Churchism had begun to appear, and the Church had drifted away from the Scriptural views of the great and good men, who, under God, laid her foundations, and framed her formularies.

The celebrated Archbishop Usher, although preferring the Episcopal form of government, says, " I have ever declared my opinion to be, that *Episcopus et Presbyter gradu tantum differunt non ordine.*"

Bishop Morton, characterised by Dr Goode as one of the most eminent and able divines of the Church of England, and who was Bishop successively of Chester, Lichfield, and Durham, thus speaks,— "Where the Bishops degenerate into wolves, there the Presbyters regain their *antient right of ordaining* (*consecrandi*.) I call it *antient*, because that the Episcopate and the Presbyterate are, *jure divino*, the same, is laid down by Marsilius, Gratian," &c. Bishop Cosin also held, that Presbyters have the intrinsic power of ordination in *actu primo*, and "that the power of ordination was restrained to Bishops, not by any absolute precept that either Christ or His Apostles gave about it, but rather by apostolic practice (?) and the perpetual custom and canons of the Church."* The language of Dr Field, one of the greatest authorities among English divines on this point, is very explicit. "It is most evident," is the conclusion he arrives at, "that wherein a Bishop excelleth a Presbyter, is not a distinct power of order, but an eminency and dignity only, specially yielded to one above all the rest of the same rank for order sake, and to preserve the unity and peace of the Church." In other words, Bishops are superior to Presbyters, not by

---

* Archbishop Potter, while asserting the superiority of the order of Bishop to that of Presbyter, admits, that "the Presbyters of Rome governed that diocese a whole year," (without a Bishop) "between the death of Fabianus and the ordination of Cornelius."

Post obitum S. Fabiani sedes vacat per unius anni, mensium iv. ac dierum xv., spatium, &c.—*Annales Cyprianicae*, (by Bishop Pearson.)—*Potter on Church Government*, p. 224.

Divine right or appointment, but by ecclesiastical arrangement, on grounds of Church order and expediency. And hence the validity of the orders of the foreign Reformed Churches, which were not Episcopal, was admitted and contended for, not only by the learned Divines of the Church of England to whom we have already referred, but also by Dean Sherlock, Bishop Andrews, Dr Sharp, Archbishop of York, Archbishops Sancroft, Wake, and Secker, and down to 1835 and 1841 by Dr Howley, the then Archbishop of Canterbury.

In a letter to the *London Guardian*, referring to the recent visit of the Archbishop of Canterbury to Inverness, and reproduced in the December number of the organ of the Scotch Episcopal Church, it is affirmed that the Church of England looks upon Presbyterian ministers in the "light of private laymen." That the Scotch Episcopal Church does so, needs no proof—the first Canon of that Church being sufficient to establish the affirmation; but that the Church of England holds the same intolerant, presumptuous, and unscriptural view, is abundantly disproved by the testimonies cited in defence of the validity of the orders of the Foreign Reformed Churches. Not only did Dr Tenison, Archbishop of Canterbury, affirm, in the debate on the Union with Scotland in 1707, that the narrow notions of all Churches had been their ruin, but, also, "that he believed the Church of Scotland to be as true a Protestant Church as the Church of England, though he could not say it was as perfect."

And so late as 1835, a letter was addressed by Archbishop Howley, in the name of himself and his "*brother bishops*" to the "Moderator of the company of pastors at Geneva, expressing their *high respect for the Protestant Churches on the Continent*," and speaking of the *Genevan Reformation* as "a noble achievement, which brought light out of darkness, and rescued their Church from the shackles of Papal domination, and the tyrannical imposition of a corrupt faith and a superstitious ritual, wrought by illustrious men who, under the direction of Almighty God, were the instruments of a happy deliverance, an event not less glorious to Geneva, than conducive to the success of the Reformation."* Besides, by the 55th Canon of 1604, the clergy of the Church of England are required to pray, in the bidding prayer before the sermon, for the Church of Scotland, which was then, as now, Presbyterian; "consequently," says Dr Goode, the Dean of Ripon,† "the very men who are now protesting against the recognition of any ordinations as valid but Episcopal, and contending that it is the doctrine of the Church of England that there is no such thing as a valid ministry but through an apostolically descended episcopate, are by Canon bound solemnly to recognise in their prayers every Sunday the existence of a valid ministry without any such ordination. For, a prayer for the Presbyterian 'Church of Scotland,' clearly involves such a recognition;" and then he (Dr Goode) proceeds to cite

---

* Goode's Rule of Faith, vol. ii., p. 323.   † Now deceased.

the well-known case of a licence having been granted in April 1582, by the Vicar-General of the Archbishop of Canterbury, with express consent and command of said Archbishop, "to John Morrison, who had only Presbyterian orders according to the laudable form and rite of the Reformed Church of Scotland," "*to celebrate divine offices, to minister the sacraments*, &c., in any convenient places in and throughout the whole province of Canterbury." Moreover, it is notorious that, between the Reformation and Restoration, many were admitted as ministers by the Church of England who had only Presbyterian ordination, and who, according to the testimony of Bishop Hall, "enjoyed spiritual promotions and livings, without any exception against the lawfulness of their calling." The validity of Presbyterian ordination is not denied in the formularies and Articles of the Church of England; but, since the Restoration the Act of Uniformity renders Episcopal ordination necessary, in order to legal institution to benefices *in England;* but the legal conditions necessary in order to *institution* do not in any way whatever alter the *doctrine* of the Church in regard to ordination.

"The old Church of England did not require re-ordination, as now done. In King Edward the Sixth's time, Peter Martyr, Martin Bucer, and P. Fagius, had ecclesiastical preferments in the Church of England; but Cranmer, whose judgment of Episcopacy we have seen before, never required re-ordination of them. He was most familiar with

Martyr, neither did he censure M. Bucer for writing that Presbyters might ordain.

"John à Lasco, with his congregation of Germans, was settled in England by Edward the Sixth's patent, he to be superintendent, and four other ministers with him; and though he wrote against some orders of the Church (of England), was with others called to reform our ecclesiastical laws.

"In Queen Elizabeth's time ordination by Presbyters was allowed, as appears by the Statute of Reformation, &c., 13 Eliz., cap. 12. It cannot refer to popish ordinations only, if at all. For—1. The words are general: Be it enacted—that every person—which doth or shall pretend to be a Priest, or minister of God's holy Word. The title of minister of God's holy Word is rarely used among the Papists, and in common use among the Reformed Churches. The ministry, with the Papists, is a real priesthood, and therefore they call their Presbyters Priests. And it is an old maxim, "Non est distinguendum ubi Lex non distinguit." 2. The subscription seems to intend those that scrupled traditions and ceremonies, which the Papists do not." *

A deputation of learned and distinguished divines of the Church of England was sent to the Synod of Dort, and took part in its deliberations; and four years before (in 1614), Royal Letters were sent by King James I. to the National Synod of the French Churches to evince his solicitude for their peace and preservation. Hooker, although a zealous Episco-

* Owen's Plea for Scripture Ordination, p. 118.

palian, makes the following concession:—" Whereas some do infer that no ordination can stand but only such as is made by Bishops which have had their ordination likewise by other Bishops before them, till we come to the very Apostles of Christ themselves—in which respect it was demanded of Beza at Poissie, by what authority he could administer the Holy Sacraments, being not thereunto ordained by any other than Calvin, &c. ? . . . . To this we answer that there may be sometimes very just and sufficient reason to allow ordination made without a Bishop."*

When Charles I. asked Archbishop Usher, "whereever he found in antiquity that Presbyters *alone ordained* any?" Usher replied, "I can show your Majesty *more*, even where *Presbyters alone successively ordained Bishops*; and instanced in Hierome's words, *Epist. ad Evagrium*, of the Presbyters of Alexandria choosing and making their own Bishops from the days of Mark till Heracles and Dionysius." Again, he says, "A Presbyter hath the *same order* in specie with a Bishop: *ergo*, a Presbyter hath *equally an intrinsic power to give orders, and is equal to him in the power of order.*" Further, he says, "I do profess that, with like affection, I should receive the blessed Sacrament at the hands of the Dutch ministers, if I were in Holland, as I should at the hands of the French ministers if I were in Charentone."†

* Book vii., chap. xiv. 11. Ed. Keble.
† Judgment of the late Archbishop of Armagh, 110-127; Life of Baxter by Sylvester, fol. lib. i., part ii., sect. 63, p. 206; Dr John Edward's Discourse on Episcopacy, chap. xiv., quoted by Powell.

The same testimony was borne by one of the most distinguished divines of the Scottish Episcopal Church, John Forbes of Corse, (Professor of Divinity in King's College, Aberdeen, in 1619, and ejected in 1640,) the learned author of "Instructiones Historico-Theologicæ de Doctrina Christiana," and well known throughout Europe as one of the most accomplished theologians of his time. In his "Irenicum amatoribus veritatis et pacis in Ecclesia Scoticana," he says, "Valida est ordinatio, quæ peragitur per Presbyteros in eis Ecclesiis, in quibus non est Episcopus . . . . habent Presbyteri de jure divino ordinandi, sicut prædicandi et baptizandi, potestatem: quamvis haec omnia exsequi debeant sub regimine et inspectione Episcopi in locis ubi est Episcopus."*

The Cyprianic age has been reckoned by Episcopalians to be their stronghold; but even then, when the rights of Presbyters were being infringed upon, Presbyters, in the absence of the Bishop, discharged all his functions. Hence we find Cyprian during his exile writing to the Presbyters, and exhorting and requesting them " to discharge their own and his office too, that so nothing might be wanting either to discipline or diligence" (Fungamini illic et vestris partibus ac meis, ut nihil vel ad disciplinam, vel ad diligentiam desit, (Epist. v., s. i., p. 15.) And again, in another epistle, he asks them, *in his stead*, (*vice mea*) to perform those offices which the ecclesiastical dispensation requires.

* Iren., lib. ii., c. xi. 13.

In an Epistle to Cyprian from Firmilian, Bishop of Cæsarea, and who was also president of the Council of Antioch, he says, " All power and grace is constituted in the Church, where Elders preside, who have the power of baptizing, confirming, and ordaining."· Qui et baptizandi, et manum imponendi, et ordinandi possident potestatem.—*Apud Cyprian Epist.* lxxv., s. vi., p. 237.

It is thus evident that, in the time of Cyprian, the intrinsic right of Presbyters to ordain was undoubted, although, by custom and ecclesiastical regulation, for the greater honour of ambitious Bishops, the right was unwarrantably curtailed.

We have already stated that one of the first, if not the first assertors of the rights of Bishops, as an *order distinct from Presbyters by divine institution*, was Dr Bancroft, in his memorable sermon at Paul's Cross in 1588; and one of the first, if not the first, " to call in question the validity of the Orders of the Foreign Non-Episcopal Churches, was Laud," in 1604 at Oxford, when taking his degree of B.D. For maintaining, on that occasion, that there could be no true Church without diocesan bishops, he was " *openly reprehended*" by Dr Holland, Regius Professor of Divinity, *for a seditious person, who would unchurch the Reformed Protestant Churches beyond seas, and now sow division between us and them who were brethren, by this* NOVEL POPISH POSITION."*

In all the ordinations which have taken place in the

* See "Goode's Rule of Faith," and "Heylin's and Prynn's Life of Laud."

Church of England, from the Reformation down to the present day, Presbyters have taken part concurrently with Bishops. By the Scotch Episcopal Church, the standing of Presbyters, in the matter of conferring ordination, is entirely taken away, and the validity of ordination by Presbyters denied; so much so, that Bishop Wordsworth, in a pastoral addressed to his clergy, declares that, " to believe that *Presbyters** alone are competent to carry on the succession of an apostolical clergy, AND TO ADMINISTER VALIDLY THE SACRAMENTS OF THE CHURCH," is to hold an article of belief, " than which there can be none more practically mischievous, or more justly excommunicable in the case of those who hold it; because there can be none which destroys more directly the essence of Christian communion." †

* *Presbyters*—" So," says the Bishop, " we must be content to call them, though, by so doing, we appear to grant the very matter in dispute."

† Pastoral Letter to his Clergy, August 1853.

CHAPTER V.

IMPORTANT DIFFERENCE IN DOCTRINE BETWEEN THE COMMUNION OFFICE OF THE CHURCH OF ENGLAND AND THAT OF THE SCOTCH EPISCOPAL CHURCH.

The Scotch Communion Office—The Invocation Prayer—Bishops Innes, Rattray, Jolly, Torry, Forbes, Skinner, Gleig—Debate in Convocation in 1862—The Bishops of Oxford, Lincoln, Llandaff.

IN the preceding chapter we pointed out the difference between the views of the Church of England and those of the Scotch Episcopal Church in regard to the validity of ordination by Presbyters, and the rights and standing of Presbyters in conferring ordination. We shall now bring before our readers the important difference in doctrine between the two Churches in regard to the sacrament of the Lord's Supper, as brought out in their communion offices respectively. All familiar with the sacramentarian controversy are aware that three widely different views have been, and still are, held in regard to the sacraments.

1. The view held by Socinians, and unjustly imputed to Zwingle, viz., that they (the sacraments) are mere "badges of profession," "naked and bare signs," and nothing more.

2. The views held by John Knox, and the Reformed Churches generally, that they are not only signs, but also *seals*,—that the sacrament of the Lord's Supper "seals the benefits of Christ's death unto true believers,"—seals not "the truth of their faith, but the *right and interest of faith*, as the seal affixed to a deed seals the right and interest of the person in the property conveyed by the deed;" or, to make use of the language of the late Principal Cunningham, "as signs they embody, in outward elements, the substance of what is set forth more fully and particularly in the written word, serving the purpose of a seal appended to a signature to a deed, not certainly as if it could very materially affect the result, so long as we had the deed and the signatures, but still operating, according to the well-known principles of our constitution, in giving some confirmation to our impressions, if not our convictions, of the reality and certainty, or reliability of the whole transaction." According to this view, which is the view given in the Westminster Standards, "The Sacraments do not, *in the first instance*, bestow grace, faith, and penitence, and are not the instruments of producing the beginnings of faith and penitence, but only confirm, increase, and seal them."* It is necessary that faith previously

* Vitringa.

exist in order to the lawful receiving of the Sacrament of the Supper, for without it the sacrament cannot be the means of ministering to the recipient's spiritual nourishment and growth in grace.

3. The doctrine held by the Church of Rome, that in the sacrament of the Lord's Supper there is a change in the elements as respects "*their substance;*" and the doctrine taught by Bishops of the Scotch Episcopal Church, that there is a change in the elements as respects "*their qualities;*" and that that change takes place, according to the Church of Rome, in virtue of the consecration of them by the Priest repeating the words of institution; and, according to the Scotch Episcopal Church, in consequence of the "Prayer of Invocation" for the Holy Spirit to descend upon *them*. (See Catechisms of Bishops Innes and Jolly.)

Also that the sacraments contain the grace which they signify, and confer it, by some *power or virtue given to them, and operating through them*. It may be also proper to state here that those who belong to the second class to which we have referred deny that there is any real presence of the *body of Christ* at the table in, with, or under either the elements, or the forms of the elements; while they firmly believe that Christ is truly present in His own ordinance to faith, and that by the indwelling of the Holy Ghost, and His gracious operations on their souls, His people are enabled to realise the presence of their Lord, and to feed upon Him by faith, after a spiritual manner, to their growth in grace and advancement in holiness.

The part of the Scotch Communion Office which has principally been objected to, as containing and setting forth doctrine essentially different from that of the Church of England and of the Reformed Churches generally, is the *Invocation Prayer*, which is as follows:—"We most humbly beseech Thee, O most merciful Father, to hear us, and of Thy almighty goodness vouchsafe to bless and sanctify, with Thy Word and Holy Spirit, these Thy gifts and creatures of bread and wine, *that they may become the body and blood of Thy most dearly beloved Son.*" It was in reference to this prayer of invocation that Lord Mackenzie, in his judgment in the case of the Rev. Sir Wm. Dunbar, Bart., *v.* Bishop Skinner of Aberdeen, delivered in the Court of Session, March 3d, 1849, said, " I cannot hold that there is *no difference* between the Scotch and English Communion Offices. I cannot overlook the circumstance that a large party of the Episcopal world think that the Communion Service of the Scotch Episcopal Church teaches the doctrine of transubstantiation. Now, as the service of the Church of England, for which Sir W. Dunbar's congregation stipulated, *excludes that*, I cannot therefore hold a matter of that kind to be unimportant."

The language of Lord Brougham in the House of Lords is even stronger and more decided. " In the Liturgy," said Lord Brougham, " promulgated by the Canons (of the Scotch Episcopal Church) the

Communion Office *varied most materially from that of the Church of England.* In the prayer called the Invocation occurred these words :—" Bless and sanctify, with Thy Word and Holy Spirit, these Thy creatures of bread and wine, that they may BECOME *the body and blood of Thy most beloved Son.*" Not— His Lordship went on to say, " become to *us* by faith for our sanctification, but that they may become—that was *absolutely*—' the body and blood of Thy most dearly beloved Son.' If this did not amount to transubstantiation, it was a very near, near approach to it—almost the nearest he (Lord Brougham) had ever seen beyond the Romish pale." (Hear, hear.) In referring to the directions given in *Skinner's Scottish Communion Office Illustrated,* in regard to the mode in which the Sacrament of the Supper is generally received in the Scotch Episcopal Church, his Lordship says that what is laid down by *Skinner* is " anything rather than Protestantism, and certainly does tend very considerably towards Romanism." The following is the statement of *Skinner* referred to by Lord Brougham :—" The practice (of administering the elements) most generally adopted in the Episcopal Church in Scotland, is that which Cyril directs, in his fifth ' Mystagogic Catechesis,' viz., that the communicant shall receive the bread in the hollow of his right hand, supported by the left, which others have called receiving the elements in the hands previously disposed in the form of a cross."

Cyril's own words are as follows :—" When you

approach, come not with the palms of your hands open, nor with the fingers separated, but put the left to below the right, as a sort of throne for it while it is to receive the King; and in the hollow of the hand receive the body of Christ, saying, Amen. Having then carefully hallowed thine eyes by the touch of so holy a body, partake. Beware, however, lest any portion should fall, for whatsoever you lose, you lose as from a member of yourself. Then, after partaking of the body of Christ, approach to the cup of His blood, not stretching forth thine hands, but looking to the ground after manner of adoration and worship, saying, Amen. Be thou then sanctified with the blood of Christ which thou takest, and while yet the moisture is on thy lips, touch it with thy hands, and hallow thine eyes and forehead and other organs of sense."

Our readers, we have no doubt, are now satisfied that, when Lord Brougham denounced the practice of administering the elements referred to with approval by Skinner, as being "anything rather than Protestantism, and certainly tending very considerably towards Romanism," his language was neither uncalled for nor unwarrantable.

We shall now examine the Scotch Communion Office in connection with expositions of the doctrine contained in it, given by Bishops of that Church, for the direction and instruction of those committed to their charge.

And first let us hear what Bishop Innes of Brechin says on the subject in his Catechism. In answer to the question, "What is the consequence of that privilege?" (viz., the effect of the Priest repeating our Saviour's words), the answer returned is, "That they (the bread and wine) are in a capacity *to be offered up to God* as the GREAT CHRISTIAN SACRIFICE."

Q. "Is this done?"

A. "Yes; the Priest immediately after makes a solemn oblation of them."

Q. "How do the bread and cup become capable of conferring all the benefits of our Saviour's death and passion?"

A. "By the Priest praying to God the Father to send His Holy Spirit upon *them*."

Q. "Are they not changed?"

A. "Yes, IN THEIR QUALITIES, but not in their substance."*

The testimony of the late Bishop Jolly is to the same effect. "Too many," says Bishop Jolly, "denied there was any *material sacrifice* whatever instituted by Christ, and left to the Church." "For this wondrous *supernatural change of the qualities of the elements* the Church always prayed, as the consummating or highest degree of their consecration, the priest solemnly invoking or calling upon God to send down His Holy Spirit upon *them*" (the elements.)*

Bishop Rattray of Dunkeld, the friend and correspondent of the Nonjurors in England—the author

---

* Innes' Cat., 1821, 26, 29, 41.

† Jolly's "Christian Sacrifice in the Eucharist," 1831.

of "Instructions concerning the Christian Covenant"—one of the most accomplished scholars of his time, and extensively conversant with the Oriental Liturgies, was one of the principal compilers and arrangers of the Scotch Communion Office. What his views in regard to the Eucharist were may be judged of by the fact that he held and taught that the same Divine Spirit by which the body of Christ was formed in the womb of the blessed Virgin, " descending on, and being united to, the elements, invigorates *them* with the virtue, power, and efficacy thereof, *and makes them one with it.*"

The views of Bishop Forbes of Brechin on the Sacrament of the Supper may be judged of by the following quotation from Cyril of Jerusalem, when expounding the meaning of the " words of Institution."—" Since, then, our Lord Jesus Christ himself has declared and said of the Bread, ' This is My Body,' who shall dare to doubt any longer? And since He has affirmed and said, ' This is My Blood,' who shall ever hesitate, saying, that it is not His blood? He once turned water into wine, in Cana of Galilee, at His own will, and is it incredible that He should have turned wine into blood? That wonderful work He miraculously wrought, when called to an earthly marriage, and shall He not much rather be acknowledged to have bestowed the fruition of His Body and Blood on the children of the bride-chamber?"*

Holding the views which the Scotch Bishops to

* Primary Charge, 1857 (2d Ed., 1858, p. 76.)

whom we have referred did, it could not be expected that they would consider the English Communion Office comparable, in point of excellence, fulness, and perfection, with the Scotch. Accordingly, we find the late Bishop Torry of Dunkeld, in a Pastoral Letter to the Clergy and Laity of his district in 1846, expressing his regret that the English Communion Office, "as it presently stands, is greatly short of its first perfection,"—that it "was shorn of its beams, and maimed, at the instigation of foreigners in the latter end of Edward the Sixth's reign;" and affirming that the Scotch Communion Office is "of a much higher and more definite character in respect of doctrine, and of much better arrangement in respect of the adjustment of its parts." "We claim," says Bishop Torry, "for our own national office the unambiguous voice of primitive truth. Bishop Forbes of Brechin, while admitting that he uses the English Office constantly himself, and that its consecration is valid, goes on to say — "As it [the English Office] stands at present, I regard it as a sad mutilation of the first office of the Reformers—as an Eucharistic service 'more marred than any;' but still, thanks be to God, preserving all the essentials of a true Sacrament."* Again, "I believe that the Scottish Office embodies the principle of primitive Christianity; that, coming, as it does, confessedly nearer to the ancient Liturgies, it bears witness not only to the two great

---

* Primary Charge, p. 57.

Christian doctrines of the *Eucharistic Sacrifice and Real Presence*," &c.

The importance attached to the Scotch Office by the Scotch Episcopal Church when agreeing to sign the Articles of the Church of England in 1804, at the Convocation held at Laurencekirk in October of that year, may be judged of by the fact that, in the address delivered on that occasion to the members of Convocation by the late Bishop Jolly, the following statement guarding and qualifying their subscription was made :—" In adopting the Articles of the Church of England and Ireland as the Articles of our Church, we must be candidly understood as taking them in unison with that book,* and not thinking any expression with regard to the Lord's Supper in the least inimical to our practice at the altar in the use of the Scotch Communion Office." "The Concordat between the Episcopal Churches of Scotland and Connecticut, signed by Bishops Kilgour (*Primus*) Petrie, John Skinner, and Seabury, also demonstrates the great importance attached to the Scotch Office, as superior to the English as it at present stands. And the conference which took place between Bishop Skinner and the Bishops of Ross and Moray previous to the consecration of Mr Torry as Bishop of Dunkeld, bears testimony to the same effect. On that occasion the following declaration was given by Mr Torry to the Bishops

---

* A Layman's Account of his Faith and Practice as a Member of the Episcopal Church in Scotland, published with the approbation of the Bishops of that Church.

in writing:—"I, the undersigned, do hereby voluntarily and *ex animo* declare, being now about to be promoted by the mercy of God to a seat in the Episcopal College of the Church of Scotland, that, when promoted to the Episcopate, I will co-operate with my colleagues in supporting a steady adherence to the truths and doctrines by which our Church has been so happily distinguished, as laid down in our excellent Communion Office, the use of which I will strenuously recommend by my own practice, and by every other means in my power. In testimony whereof I have signed this declaration at Aberdeen, 12th October, 1808. PAT. TORRY."

That declaration he had ever in view; and we find him, in his eighty-third year, making a solemn appeal to his clergy on behalf of that office which he loved so well. "I tremble," says the aged Bishop, " I tremble for the stability of our humble Zion if ever the day shall arrive when the claims of the Scotch Communion Office to primary authority and general use shall not be manfully upheld. It is painful to think with what indifference those who are loudest in their cry for the exclusive use of the English Office, view the indignity thereby offered to the memory of those distinguished prelates to whose faithful labours this Church owes a debt of gratitude which it can never adequately repay."

A declaration to the same effect was demanded by Bishop Skinner from Dr Gleig of Stirling, as a condition of the consent of the Primus to Dr Gleig's promotion to the Bishopric of Brechin. In answer to Bishop Skinner's letter, Dr Gleig expressed his readiness to subscribe and deliver a declaration similar to that which had been given by Bishop Torry, stating, at the same time, that he was much attached to the Scottish Communion Office, and maintaining "its superiority over the English form."

While the older Bishops, the fathers of the Scotch Episcopal Church, survived, the Scotch Communion Office maintained the position which it had so long occupied as of "primary authority;" but by a canon drawn up, we believe, by Bishop Wordsworth, and passed by a General Synod in 1863, the Scotch Communion Office is no longer of primary authority, although its use is still canonically permitted. The present Bishops of the Scotch Episcopal Church were for the most part, previous to their elevation, clergymen of the Church of England. Their sympathies and predilections were all in favour of the *Book of Common Prayer*. They were most desirous of being as closely connected with the Church of England as possible, and to enjoy the advantages which such a connection would confer; and, finding that the Scotch Communion Office was one great barrier in the way of their being favourably regarded by English clergymen, they exerted themselves strenuously to alter the canons so that that office, while permitted, would no longer be of primary authority. That it was a great hindrance is unquestionable; for not only did the Bishop of Cashel, in his letters to Bishop Low in 1845, maintain that the Scotch

Episcopal Church held doctrine, in her Communion Office, which differed little, if at all, from the transubstantiation of the Church of Rome,—that her "Prayer-Book goes back towards Popery in a degree for which *she has no precedent* in the formularies of any Reformed Church;" but further, that if his opinion were asked by ministers who had received their orders from the English Church, but who were ministering to congregations of the Scotch Episcopal Church, he would feel constrained to say, "Come out from her and be separate."

Of the existence of this deep-rooted feeling of aversion on the part of the Bishops of the Church of England to the Scotch Communion Office, unmistakeable evidence was afforded so late as 1862, in a discussion which took place in the Upper House of Convocation on the Scotch Episcopal Church, in the course of which the Bishops of Oxford, Lincoln, and Llandaff objected to the office in the strongest terms, affirming that the existence of that office was one of the greatest barriers to a recognition of the Scotch Episcopal Church by the Church of England.

So important does the Bishop of Oxford believe the points of difference between the English and Scotch Offices to be, that he felt unable, when in Scotland a few years ago, to take part in the Communion Service on one occasion when the Scotch Office was to be used, and rose and left the church before that part of the service commenced.

In the debate in Convocation in 1862, the Bishop

of Lincoln spoke as follows :—" The present Scotch service is neither that of Edward VI. nor that which was drawn up for them by Laud, but an entirely different one, altered in many important points, and drawn up by some who dissented from our Church—being Nonjurors—in that precise form and manner, because they wished to embody therein their opinion as to the defects—or, as they term them, the errors—of the English Communion Service; it has therefore been regarded as a standing protest against the Communion Service of the Church of England. Looking at it in that light, it can be no great matter of surprise that there is an unwillingness on the part of many members of the Church of England to receive at once into equal communion those who not merely entertain a different opinion with reference to the most solemn service of the Church, but are also bound to hold it of primary authority by a canon passed as recently as 1838. There it stands upon the statute-book, a solemn ordinance of the Church of Scotland, although an office which history teaches us was drawn up *as a protest against our own*, which is thought to contain passages altered most injuriously for doctrinal purposes, and in order to make a distinct difference between the two services."

On the same occasion the Bishop of Llandaff made the following statement :—" Whether the idea is correct or incorrect, I do not now undertake to say; but, as the Bishop of Oxford has candidly admitted, the fact is that there is a deeply-rooted feeling in the minds of a large portion of the English Church that there are differences that *are essential*, both in the way of omission and in the way of particular expressions, between the two services."

Our readers will now have no difficulty in perceiving why Bishop Wordsworth, and his brother Bishops, many of whom, like himself, received their orders from the English Church, were so desirous of altering the Canon " of Holy Communion," in order to be allowed to bask in the sunshine of the favour of the Church of England.

Notwithstanding, however, the alteration made by the Canon of 1863, the Scotch Episcopal Church is still responsible for the doctrine contained in, and taught by, the Scotch Communion Office; for, in the amended Canon, that office is said to have " been long adopted and extensively used, under the guidance of divers learned and orthodox Bishops ;" and, by the same Canon, " it is hereby enacted, that the adoption of the Book of Common Prayer as the Service Book of this Church shall not affect the practice of the congregations of this Church which now use the said Scotch Communion Office."

In addition to the doctrine of Bishop Rattray, already referred to, in regard to the descent of the Divine Spirit on the elements, and the effect of that descent, he also held that the oblation of the Sacrament of the Supper is to be offered up, not only on behalf of the *living*, but also of the *dead*. " Then the priest," says Bishop Rattray, " maketh intercession, in virtue of this sacrifice thus offered up, in commemoration of our *union with* the one great personal sacrifice of Christ, for the whole Catholic Church, and pleadeth the merits of this one sacrifice in behalf of all estates and conditions of men in it, offering the memorial thereof not for the *living only*, but for the *dead also*, in commemoration of the patriarchs, prophets, apostles, martyrs, and of all the saints who have pleased God, in their several generations, from the beginning of the world; and for rest, light, and peace, and a blessed resurrection, and *a merciful trial*, in the day of the Lord, *to all the faithful departed*.

Bishop Rattray's views may also be learned from "The Ancient Liturgy of the Church of Jerusalem," prepared by him in Greek and English, "with additions from the Scottish Office of 1637, and rubrics suited to modern times and uses." Said Liturgy was published after his death in 1744. In the Oblation and Invocation Prayers we have the following:—"We sinners offer to Thee, O Lord, this tremendous and unbloody sacrifice, beseeching Thee that Thou wouldest not deal with us after our sins, nor reward us after our iniquities," &c., &c. Again, after the prayer, "Grant that we may all find mercy and favour with all Thy saints, who from the beginning of the world have pleased Thee in their several generations, [particularly *N*, whom we this day commemorate,"] it is said, "*Here the priest shall pause a while, he and the people secretly recommending those departed whom each thinks proper.*

"*And then the priest shall go on as follows:—*

"Remember, O Lord, the God of spirits and of all flesh, those whom we have remembered, and those also whom we have not remembered, from righteous Abel even unto this day: Do Thou give them rest in the region of the living, in the bosoms of our holy fathers, *Abraham, Isaac*, and *Jacob*, whence sorrow, grief, and lamentation are banished away, where the light of Thy countenance visits and shines continually; and vouchsafe to bring them to Thy heavenly kingdom."

Bishop W. Abernethy Drummond, of Edinburgh, in writing to the Bishop of Dunkeld, says:—"I pray you to beg the clergy to give me the benefit of their prayers, and bid them also put me in their distich when I am gone (I trust) to a better world;" and the Rev. J. Skinner, in his Scotch Communion Office Illustrated, states that the *Eucharist Oblation* is particularly adapted as an intercession on behalf of the departed faithful.

Bishop Jolly's testimony is to the same effect:—

"Need we," asks Bishop Jolly, "apply to the saints in paradise for their prayers?

"*A.* No; they know our dangerous condition here, and their charity wants not to be desired to recommend us to God.

"*Q.* Why do we pray for them?

"*A.* Because their present condition is imperfect, and therefore capable of improvement, and because they are to be judged at the last day, and will then stand in need of mercy."—*Jolly's Catechism*, 1829.

The same doctrine was also taught by Bishop John Skinner, who, for a long period, was *Primus* of the Scotch Episcopal Church.

In answer to the question, "How is this Communion," viz., the Communion between "the Church on earth and the saints in paradise," "maintained or kept up?" we have the following reply:—"As far as we know, by mutual prayer and thanksgiving; *they*, no doubt, praying for our salvation, *we* blessing God for their good example, wishing the increase of their happiness, and praying for the hastening of His kingdom, that we, with all those that are departed in the true faith of His holy name, may have our perfect consummation and bliss, both in body and soul, in God's everlasting glory."—*Skinner's Catechism*, 1799-1837.

In harmony with the above are the views of the learned author of "The Christian Sacrifice in the Eucharist," the Rev. George Hay Forbes of Burntisland. They are embodied in the following propositions:—

I. "That the Eucharist is a material sacrifice.

II. "That the bread and wine become the body and blood of Christ, through the operation of the Holy Ghost.

III. "That the Eucharist is a SIN-OFFERING, as well as a thank-offering, and that the benefits thereof are applied, not to the living only, but also to the *faithful departed*."*

Accordingly, to bring their Communion Office

---

* Christian Sacrifice in the Eucharist, Part I., p. 22.

into more perfect harmony with their doctrine in regard to prayers for the dead, they altered the Office of 1636-7, (Laud's Service Book.) In that Office, as in the Church of England, the following words occur:—" Let us pray for the whole state of Christ's Church militant here on earth." These important words of limitation, "*militant here on earth,*" *they have erased,* in order to embrace in their prayers the *dead* as well as the living, and have also transposed the prayer which originally was offered *before* the oblation, the words of institution, and the consecration prayer, and have placed it *after* the oblation and consecration prayer. This is considered to be the most perfect " arrangement of the parts " of the Communion Office; because, after the " tremendous and unbloody sacrifice " has been offered up to God, and He has thereby been propitiated, then is the proper time to present, in connection with it, our supplications before Him on behalf both of the living and of the dead; or, as the author of the Christian Sacrifice in the Eucharist expresses it, " the propitiations for the Church militant on earth, *and requiescent in Hades.*" *

* Christian Sacrifice in the Eucharist, Part I., p. 21.

CHAPTER VI.

SOURCES FROM WHICH THE SCOTCH COMMUNION OFFICE HAS BEEN DERIVED.

The Missal—Fragmenta Liturgica—Principal Baillie—Hallam—The Oriental Liturgies—The Greek Church.

WE come now to examine the *Scotch Communion Office*, in connection with the sources from which it has been derived, viz., the Roman Missal, on the one hand, and the Oriental Liturgies on the other.

In the preface to his *Fragmenta Liturgica*, vol. i., the Rev. T. Hall affirms that " the Scottish Office is the Romish Missal, just as is the English Office, —that is, the Missal reformed and restored to the condition most consonant, in the judgment of either Church (for here the Churches differ) with the formularies of primitive antiquity. The English Office (as it now stands) was arranged from the earlier Offices of Edward, Elizabeth, and James; as these had been arranged before by a comparison of the Missal with the Primitive Liturgies, and a subjection of both to the testimony of the Word of God.

.... The reason for the variations that appear in the result is probably this, that Scripture has prevailed more over tradition in the southern (the English) Office, and tradition more over Scripture in the northern," (the Scottish.) Mr Hall's statement can only be taken with important qualifications. It is no doubt true that the English Office was arranged from the earlier Offices of Edward, Elizabeth, and James; but Mr Hall omits to state that the English Reformers, fearing lest an improper use might be made of certain expressions in the first Communion Office of Edward VI., carefully revised it; removing everything which had a Popish tendency, or that countenanced the opinions that in the Sacrament of the Supper there was either a true propitiatory sacrifice, or intercession for the faithful departed; while the Scotch Episcopal Church, instead of being satisfied with Laud's Service Book, which, in point of doctrine, was substantially the same as the first Office of Edward VI., substituted for it an Office of a still more objectionable nature. The points of resemblance between Laud's Service Book and the Roman Missal have been graphically brought out by Baillie, Principal of the Glasgow University, 1641, in his "*Parallel or brief comparison of the Scottish Liturgy with the Mass Book, the Breviary, the Ceremonial, and other Romish rituals, wherein is clearly and shortly demonstrated that the (Scottish) Liturgy is taken for the most part, word by word, out of those Antichristian writs,*" &c. In his preface, Principal Baillie says,—" With the Liturgy of the Church of England I will not meddle. It is my only intention to consider the Scottish Liturgy, which the Scottish Bishops persuade the king (Charles the First) to be all one with the English. I will show that this our Service Book is taken, well near word for word, out of the sinks of Rome." Again, "The main portion of the Offertory is the placing of the bread and wine upon the altar, and the offering of them up to God, even before the consecration, with certain prayers to be a peace-offering, that so they may be fitted for the matter of the propitiatory sacrifice following." The Church of England, detesting this abuse, plucked it up by the root, and put it far away from their Book, (Liturgy;) but our men (the Scottish Bishops) have put it in on us in express terms," p. 32. "As for the offering of these oblations and prayers for the benefit not only of the quick, but of the dead, we see that after they have commended their oblations to be mercifully received of God, and put to their back prayers for the good of the *living* in all degrees and callings, they immediately subjoin 'not only their thanksgivings, but their prayers and supplications for the *dead*, even for the salvation of their soul.' As the Roman mass referred to the oblation of bread and wine, and the offertory prayers upon it, to the honour of saints in heaven, to the benefit of the living, and good of the faithful who are dead, in whatever place they be, whether in heaven or elsewhere, so does our (the Scottish Service) Book. But no ways the English. They speak not of the benefit of the dead; and the blessings they crave to the living *have no reference at all to the oblation of bread and wine:* for they have plucked up by the root that pestiferous weed which yet our men have planted again in the old place, and put to the back of it our offertory prayer, after the manner of the Roman mass," p. 36. "Among the omissions in the Scottish Liturgy none are more complained of than the deleting of these words of the English Liturgy in the delivery of the bread at the sacramental table,—'and eat this in remembrance that Christ died for thee, and feed on Him in thine heart by faith, with thanksgiving,'—a passage destructive to transubstantiation, as diverting communicants from carnal manducation, and directing their souls to a spiritual repast on their Saviour; all which, in the Scottish Liturgy, is cut off."—*Fuller's Church History of Britain,* 1655, pp. 161, 162.

Hallam, and Malcolm Laing, testify to the same effect as Principal Baillie. "The English model," says Hallam, "was not closely followed; the variations having all a tendency towards the Romish worship."* "Unfortunately," says Laing, "in receding from the English service, these minute alterations approached proportionably to the Romish Missal."†

But while there exist numerous resemblances in form and in doctrine between the Roman Missal and the Scotch Communion Office, there can be no doubt that one of the distinctive objectionable

* Hallam, *Const. Hist.*, iii., 427. † Laing, i., 115.

features of that Office, as it now stands, viz., the "Invocation Prayer," has been derived from the Liturgies of the Eastern, not of the Western Church. Accordingly, we find that Bishop Torry, in his Pastoral Letter, published in 1846, refers the clergy and laity in his district to the Primitive Oriental Eucharistic Offices as the sources from which said Invocation Prayer and Offices have been derived. In regard to the Invocation Prayer, it is of importance, at the outset, to have the true state of the question set forth,—to have clear and distinct views as to the precise point at issue between the defenders of the Scotch Communion Office, and those who take exception to the part of it now under consideration. It is not a Prayer of Invocation for the descent of the Holy Spirit to which exception is taken, but to the special form of it contained in the Scotch Office, viz., a Prayer of Invocation of the Holy Spirit, not that the faith of the communicant may be increased, and that all his graces may be in lively exercise; but a prayer for the descent of the Holy Ghost *upon the elements of bread and wine, " supernaturally changing their qualities," in virtue of which change they* " BECOME THE BODY AND BLOOD OF CHRIST."

As regards Bishop Torry's reference to the " Primitive Eucharist Offices," it is of importance to remember that there is not the shadow of a reason for supposing that any of these Liturgies existed before the third century. None of them existed before that period, and therefore their value, as evidence of the views held in regard to the nature and design of the Lord's Supper, in the apostolic age, is worthless.

The most ancient of these Liturgies, viz., the Clementine, is also the most simple, and the most free from error. Bishop Torry, in his Pastoral Letter of 1846, says of it:—" The Clementine, in reference to the consecration of the sacramental elements, speaks thus,—' Send down thy Holy Spirit, that He may *make* this bread the body of thy Christ, and this cup the blood of thy Christ.'" The Bishop does not profess to quote from the Liturgy itself, but refers to the works of Brett and Bingham, as the sources from which he derived his information. The translation, however, as given by the Bishop, is stronger than is warranted by the copy of the Greek text which now lies before us, in which the invocation is as follows:—" Καὶ καταπέμψης τὸ ἅγιόν σου Πνεῦμα, &c., ὅπως ἀποφήνῃ τὸν ἄρτον τοῦτον σῶμα τοῦ Χριστοῦ σου, &c. &c." "Send down thy Holy Spirit that He may *make manifest* this bread as the body of thy Christ, and this cup as the blood of thy Christ."

In the Liturgies of St James and St Mark the language employed is stronger. The words "*make* this bread the holy body of thy Christ," &c., are used instead of, as in the Clementine Liturgy, "*make manifest* this bread as the body of thy Christ,"— ποιήσῃ being used in the one case, and ἀποφήνῃ in the other.

When we come down to the later Liturgies of St Chrysostom and St Basil, we find greater differences still, forms of expression which seem to teach and set forth a change of the elements by the descent of the Holy Spirit upon them. The invocation in the Liturgy of St Chrysostom is as follows:—" Moreover we offer to thee this reasonable and unbloody service, and we entreat, and beseech, and supplicate thee, send down the Holy Spirit on us, and on these gifts lying before us, and make ($\pi o i \eta \sigma o \nu$) this bread the precious body of thy Christ, and that which is in this cup the precious blood of thy Christ, having changed them ($\mu \varepsilon \tau \alpha \beta \alpha \lambda \grave{\omega} \nu$) by thy Holy Spirit." The invocation in the Liturgy of St Basil is substantially the same as in that of St Chrysostom. The words having changed them (that is, the elements) also occur, the only difference being, that instead of " make this bread the precious body of thy Christ," we have " constitute ($\grave{\alpha} \nu \alpha \delta \varepsilon \tilde{i} \xi \alpha \iota$) this bread the very precious body of our Lord and God and Saviour, Jesus Christ." Of the Jacobite or Syrian Church, and the Armenian Church, suffice to say, that they both reject the doctrine of the Orthodox Churches regarding the union of two distinct natures in the person of Christ, recognising only the decrees of the first three general councils. They deny the procession of the Holy Ghost from the Son. They maintain the doctrine of the transmutation of the elements, in virtue of consecration, into the Body and Blood of Christ, the invocation of the Virgin Mary, and of saints and angels, the worship of the cross and pictures, the offering of a propitiatory sacrifice in the Eucharist, and prayers for the dead.

The same also may be affirmed substantially of the Coptic and Abyssinian Churches. Whether the language of the three earliest Liturgies teaches and sets forth the doctrine of the "Real Objective Presence," in virtue of the Invocation Prayer, or merely a relative change in the elements—a change in use and purpose—the strength of the language employed being accounted for by the fact that the fathers were in the habit of calling the signs by the names of the things signified by them—a habit justified by scriptural precedents, as, "That rock was Christ," "I am the vine," "The seven kine are seven years," "This is my body," &c., &c., may be matter of uncertainty; but of this there can be no doubt, that in the Greek Church now the language is not employed to denote a relative change, but a change amounting to a transubstantiation of the elements. The Oriental Church to which, from the time of the Non-jurors' correspondence with it to the present day, the Scotch Episcopal Church, as well as the Puseyite party in the Church of England, look with reverence, and with which they earnestly desire to be united is, as we stated in a former chapter, that which arrogates to itself the lofty appellation of the "One Holy Catholic and Apostolic Church of the Orthodox," or the Orthodox Eastern Church, best known by the name of "The Greek Church." If the Scotch Communion Office, then, is derived from the Oriental Churches, it will be of importance to ascertain what are the doctrines held and taught by the principal Oriental Church—the Orthodox Eastern

Church, the chief bishop of which is the Patriarch of Constantinople, and of which the Russian Church forms part. With a view to this, I shall refer more particularly to two Confessions of Faith :—1st, That approved by the Synod of Jassy in 1643, and attested by the four patriarchs, and called the Orthodox Confession of Faith of the Catholic and Apostolic Eastern Church, which Confession every pious and Orthodox Christian, who is a member of the Eastern and Apostolical Church, is, by "unanimous and synodical sentence, ordained to read and to receive." The second Confession was put forth by the Jerusalem Synod held at Bethlehem in 1672 by Dositheus the Patriarch of Jerusalem, and hence called the "Confession of Dositheus," and was afterwards approved by the four patriarchs and their clergy.

In regard to the Sacrament of the Lord's Supper, the Confessions above referred to teach, firstly, the doctrine of a transmutation of the elements into the true body and blood of Christ; and, secondly, that in the Eucharist there is a propitiatory sacrifice offered for the quick and the dead. "The substance of the bread is changed into the substance of the holy body of Christ, (μεταβάλλεται εἰς τὴν οὐσίαν), and the substance of the wine into the substance of His precious blood." "On which account we ought to honour and worship, with the worship of *Latria*, the holy Eucharist, *in the same way* as (ὁμοίως καθὼς) our Saviour Jesus himself." "After these words" (the Invocation Prayer for the descent of the Spirit upon the elements) "the transubstantiation (ἡμετουσίωσις) immediately takes place, and the bread is changed into the true body of Christ, and the wine into His true blood. The forms only by which they are visible to the sight remain, and that by divine appointment." (Orthodox Confess., Pt. I.; Resp. 107, pp. 180, 181.)

"In the celebration of this Sacrament," says the Confession of Dositheus, (Decr. 17, pp. 457, 456, 463), "we believe that our Lord Jesus Christ is present, not figuratively, nor by a representation, nor by superabounding grace, but truly and actually, so that after the consecration of the bread and wine the bread is changed, transubstantiated, converted, transformed into the true body of our Lord, which was born in Bethlehem of the ever-virgin, was baptized in Jordan, suffered, was buried, rose again, ascended, sits at the right hand of God the Father, and will come at a future time in the clouds of heaven; and the wine is converted and transubstantiated into the very true blood of our Lord, which, when He hung upon the cross, was poured out for the life of the world. Moreover, we believe that the very body and blood of the Lord, which are in the sacrament of the Eucharist, ought to be honoured with supreme honour, and worshipped with the worship of *Latria*, (the highest degree of worship.) Those who violate this doctrine, the Catholic Church of Christ rejects and anathematises," (Confess. Decr. 17, pp. 457, 463.)

That a propitiatory sacrifice is offered in the

Sacrament of the Lord's Supper for the living and the dead is plainly taught and set forth in the two Confessions already referred to. "This Sacrament," says the Orthodox Confession, "is a propitiation and means of reconciliation with God for our sins, both of the living and the dead. It is certain that many sinners are freed from the chains of Hades, not by their own repentance or confession, as Scripture says, (Ps. vi. 5), 'For in Hades who shall confess to thee?' but by the good works of the living, and the prayers of the Church for them, and chiefly by the unbloody sacrifice, which the Church daily offers for all the living and the dead in common," (Confess., Resp. 107, pp. 183, 184; also, Pt. i., Resp. 64, pp. 132, 133.) "We believe," says the Confession of Dositheus, "that the Eucharist is a true and propitiatory sacrifice offered up for all the pious, both living and dead, and for the benefit of all," (Confess., Decr. 17, p. 461.)

In addition to the views above referred to regarding the *Eucharist*, the two Confessions also set forth the following doctrines:—1. That the rule of faith is composed of tradition as well as of Scripture, and not of Scripture alone. 2. That the books of Ecclesiasticus, Judith, Tobit, Bel and the Dragon, &c., are canonical books of Scripture. 3. The septenary number of the sacraments. 4. Prayers for the dead. 5. The hyperdulic worship of the Virgin Mary. 6. The dulic worship of angels and saints. 7. The adoration of the Cross. 8. The denial of the Scriptures to the people.

1. In regard to the Rule of Faith—All Protestant and Evangelical Churches maintain that the Word of God, as contained in the Scriptures of the Old and New Testaments, is the only infallible and authoritative rule in matters of Faith; but the Greek Church not less than the Church of Rome, holds that the Rule of Faith is composed of Tradition conjointly with Scripture. On this point, the Orthodox Confession, the Confession of Dositheus, and the Synodical Letter of the Synod of Jerusalem, are full and explicit. Referring to 2 Thess. ii. 15, the Orthodox Confession says, "It is manifest that the Articles of the Faith have their authority and proof partly from the Holy Scripture, partly from the Tradition of the Church, and from the teaching of Synods and Holy Fathers." And again: "Some (doctrines) are delivered by the Scripture, which are contained in the divine books of the Holy Scriptures; and there are other doctrines which were delivered orally by the Apostles, and these were declared by the Synods and Holy Fathers. AND OUR FAITH IS FOUNDED UPON THESE TWO,"—καὶ εἰς τὰ δύο ταῦτα ἡ πίστις εἶναι τεθεμελιωμένη. (Confess., Pt. I., Resp. 4, pp. 59, 60.) "We believe," says the Confession of Dositheus, "that the witness of the Catholic Church possesses no less authority than the Divine Scripture; for one and the same Holy Spirit being the author of both, it is altogether equivalent to be taught by the Scripture, and by the Catholic Church. (Confess., Decr. 2, p. 427.) I may also add that the

Apocryphal books are held as forming part of the Canonical books of divine revelation.

2. The Greek Church, not less than the Church of Rome, prohibits the general use of the Scriptures by the people. "Scripture," says the Confession of Dositheus, "is not to be read by all, but only by those who dive into the depths of the Spirit with suitable earnestness of investigation, and who know in what ways the divine Scripture is to be searched, and taught, and read. But to those who are inexperienced, and interpret the Scriptures without discrimination, or only according to the letters, or in any other way foreign from piety, the Catholic Church, knowing by experience the bad effects, prohibits the reading. So that it is permitted to every pious person to hear the Scriptures; but to read some parts of the Scripture, and particularly of the Old Testament, is forbidden for the aforesaid and other similar reasons." (Confess., Q., et., R. 1, pp. 465, 466.)

3. In regard to the number of the Sacraments, the Orthodox Confession contains the following statement: "The seven Sacraments of the Church are these, Baptism, the Unguent of Chrism, the Eucharist, Penance, Priesthood, honourable Marriage, and anointing with oil with prayer." Again, from the same Confession, a Sacrament is "a ceremony which, under a certain visible form, acts as a cause, and brings into the soul of the faithful the invisible grace of God, instituted by our Lord, by which each of the faithful receives the divine grace." (Confess.,

Pt. 1, Resp. 98, 99.) "When the priest anoints the baptized person with the holy ointment, the gifts of the Holy Spirit are poured out upon him." (Confess., Resp. 104, p. 176.)

4. In regard to the worship of the Virgin Mary, the Orthodox Confession says, "Every orthodox Christian ought to seek the intercession of the Virgin, for the intercession of the Mother is of much avail to obtain the good will of the Son; and every one who desires to pay proper respect to her will recite the invocations and hymns of the Church, composed in her praise." (Confess., Pt. 1, Resp, 42, pp. 110, 111.) "We believe," says the Confession of Dositheus, "that Jesus Christ our Lord is the only Mediator, but we say that in our prayers and petitions to Him the saints are our intercessors, and before all the Immaculate Mother of that very God, the Word, and the holy angels, to whose guardianship also we know that we are committed." (Confess., Decr. 8, p. 234.) "We honour the saints with two different kinds of honour: the Mother of God, the Word, with one kind, which we call *hyperdulic*. For inasmuch as she is truly the servant of the one God, nay, even Mother, as having brought forth in the flesh one of the Persons of the Trinity, therefore she is extolled as beyond all comparison, excelling all the angels and saints, whence also we assign to her hyperdulic worship." (ὑπερδουλικὴν τὴν προσκύνησιν.) (Confess., Quæst. 4, pp. 468, 469.) "To the Mother of God let us poor sinners earnestly run and fall down before her, crying repentantly from

the depth of our soul, O Lady, help, having compassion upon us; hasten, we perish under a multitude of sins; turn not thy servants away empty; for thou art the alone hope ($μόνην \ ελπίδα$) we possess." The last extract is taken from the " Service of the Paracletical Canon to the most holy Mother of God," p. 576, as inserted in the Euchologium.

5. In regard to the mediation and worship of saints. "We maintain," says the Confession of Dositheus, "that the saints are our intercessors and mediators with God, not only when upon earth, but more especially after death, when their eyes being opened and they clearly behold the Holy Trinity, its infinite light impresses upon their minds the things which concern us." (Confess., Decr. 8, p. 435.) "With the second kind of worship, which we call dulic, we worship—that is, we honour—the holy angels, apostles, prophets, martyrs, and, in a word, all the saints."

The following from page 90 of the Paracletical Service book, is one out of many prayers to the saints: "O father Nicholas, give me liberation from all my ills by thy intercessions; O blessed, by thy supplications to thy Master, save me, O blessed of God, for I call thee my patron; and send down Thy aid, O Father, to me who call upon Thee."

6. In regard to the worship of pictures, images, and the cross, the Greek Church does not permit the worship of *graven* images or idols; but she does permit and enjoin the adoration of "icons"—that is, of pictures or representations of things which

really exist. "An icon," says the Orthodox Confession, is "a representation which represents a true thing, which has an existence in the world; as the icon of our Saviour Christ, and of the Virgin Mary, and of all the saints." What, then, is the doctrine of the Greek Church in regard to the adoration of icons and of the cross?

"Moreover," says the Confession of Dositheus, "we worship and honour the wood of the precious life-giving cross upon which our Saviour wrought His world-redeeming passion, as also the figure of the life-giving cross, the manger at Bethlehem, the place of Calvary, the life-bearing sepulchre, and the other holy objects of worship; moreover, the sacred Gospels, and the sacred vessels by which the unbloody sacrifice is performed. We also worship, and honour, and kiss the icon of our Lord Jesus Christ, and the most holy Mother of God, and all the saints; as also of the holy angels, as they were seen by some of our forefathers and prophets. And we represent the most Holy Spirit as He was seen in the form of a dove." (With the seventh holy Œcumenical Synod), "we anathematize those that worship either a saint, or angel, or icon, with the worship of *latria*, and we give the worship of *latria* to the Triune God alone. And we also anathematize those that say that the worship of icons is idolatry, or that do not worship them, and that do not honour the Cross and the Saints, according to the tradition of the Church." (Confess, Resp. 4, pp. 468-474.) The following invocations are taken from the Horologium, pp. 519-

524: "O thrice-blessed and most reverend Cross! we, the faithful, worship and magnify thee, rejoicing in thy divine exaltation: hail, blessed wood." "O Cross! the beginning of salvation; O Cross! the joy of martyrs, protect, shield, and guard those that boast in thy strength." Many more extracts might easily be given. I shall, however, only add, in regard to the doctrines held by the Greek Church, that the procession of the Holy Ghost from the Father and the Son is denounced as heresy.

We are aware that the Russian Church has assumed a degree of independence, in various ways, which her priests and her members would find it difficult to reconcile with her position as an integral portion of the "one Holy Catholic and Apostolic Church of the Orthodox."

In her chief Bishop, the late lamented Philaret, Patriarch of Moscow, she had a man of amiable disposition, of fervent piety, and to some extent of enlightened views; just as, from time to time, we have had, in the Church of Rome, men like Fenelon, and Pascal, and Martin Boos, who have risen greatly above the doctrines taught by their Church; but still it is not to the opinions of individual men, however eminent, that we are to look in endeavouring to ascertain the real doctrines of a Church, but to her own authoritative formularies and standards, the only reliable sources of information upon the subject. *

* Appendix Note.

CHAPTER VII.

THE REFORMED CHURCHES AND THE DOCTRINE OF THE SACRAMENTS.

Scotch Confession of 1560—Craig's Catechism, 1592—Synod of London, 1552—Articles of the Church of England—The Continental Reformed Churches—Zwingle—The Zurich Confession—Consensus Tigurinus—The Belgic and Gallican Confessions—Cranmer — Ridley — Athanasius — Augustine — Communion Service of the Church of England for the Sick.

THE doctrine of the Reformed Churches, in regard to the Sacrament of the Lord's Supper, while differing widely from that taught by the Church of Rome, the Greek Church, and the Scotch Episcopal Bishops, to whom reference has been made, also differed widely from the low views entertained of that ordinance by the Socinians or Remonstrants, who taught that the sacraments are mere badges of profession, and nothing more. In opposition to these views, we have the following explicit statement in the Scottish Confession of 1560, commonly called John Knox's Confession:—"We utterly condemn the vanity of those who affirm sacraments to be nothing else but naked and bare signs." And the Westminster Confession, while stating that one object of a sacrament is "to put a visible difference between those that belong unto the Church and the rest of the world, and solemnly to engage them to the service of God in Christ," and is thus a badge of profession, declares, at the same time, that "sacraments are holy signs and seals of the covenant of grace immediately instituted by God to represent Christ and His benefits, and to confirm our interest in Him." In the catechism prepared by John Craig, the friend and colleague of Knox, which catechism was drawn up by order of the General Assembly, and sanctioned by that venerable body in 1592, we have the following :—" Ques. 71. *What signifieth the action of the Supper?* Ans. That our souls are fed spiritually by the body and blood of Jesus Christ. Ques. 72. *When is this done?* Ans. When we feel the efficacy of His death in our conscience by the Spirit of faith." And in opposition to the views of the "real objective presence," we have "Ques. 75. *Is Christ's body in the elements?* Ans. No, but it is in heaven. (Acts i. 11.) Ques. 76. *Why, then, is the element called His body?* Ans. Because it is a sure seal of His body given to our souls."

The Synod of London, held in 1552, in their articles which received the sanction of Edward VI., condemned alike the Romish doctrine of transubstantiation and the Lutheran doctrine of consubstantiation, and taught that none of the faithful "should believe or profess a real and corporeal presence of the body and blood of Christ in the Eucharist." In opposition to the Romish doctrine, "that the sacraments contain the grace which they signify," and confer it "*ex opere operato*, or by some sort of physical or intrinsic power bestowed upon them, apart from the state of mind of the recipient, and that the Lord's Supper invariably conveys spiritual nourishment," the Synod of London declares, "To those who receive it worthily and with faith, the bread which we break is the communion of the body of Christ." The language of Articles xxv. and xxviii. of the Church of England is equally explicit. "In such only," says Article xxv., "as worthily receive the sacraments, they have a wholesome effect or operation; but they that receive them unworthily, purchase to themselves damnation, as St Paul saith." And again, Article xxviii., "The body of Christ is given, taken, and eaten in the Supper, only after an heavenly and spiritual manner. And the mean whereby the body of Christ is received and eaten in the Supper is faith."

The doctrine taught by the Continental Reformed Churches on the nature and design of the sacraments is substantially the same as that which was held and taught by the Scottish Reformers.

In Article xvii. of his Sixty-seven Articles, of date 1523, Zwingle says, "Christ who offered Himself once upon the cross is the eternally sufficient offering and sacrifice for the sins of all believers. Whence it follows that the mass is not a sacrifice, but the commemoration of the sacrifice made upon the cross, and, as it were, a seal of the redemption effected by Christ." Again, in the "Expositio Chr. Fidei," he says, "The natural substantial body of Christ, in which He suffered, and in which He is now seated in heaven, at the right hand of God, is not in the Lord's Supper eaten corporeally, or as to its essence, but spiritually only." And again, "We assert, therefore, that the body of Christ is not eaten in the Supper in a gross carnal manner as the Papists pretend, but spiritually and sacramentally, with a devout, believing, and holy mind, as St Chrysostom says."

The ministers of the Church of Zurich, in their "Sincere Confession," of date 1545, declare that, to believe on Christ, very God and very man crucified for us, is truly to eat the bread of Christ; that "to believe is to eat; and to eat is to believe;" being precisely the same doctrine which was taught by Augustine centuries before. In 1549, Calvin, representing the Genevan Church, proceeded to Zurich to confer with Bullinger, the successor of Zwingle. A common understanding was come to, by which the views of the Genevan and Swiss Churches, on the subject of the sacraments, were brought into a state of perfect agreement, and the result was the publication of the Consensus Tigurinus, consisting of twenty-six articles. The views set forth in these articles are substantially the same as those taught in the Westminster Standards, and the Larger and Shorter Catechisms, and are in direct opposition to transubstantiation, the adoration of the host, and the local presence of the body of Christ in the Supper. The same may be said of the Heidelberg Catechism, sanctioned in 1563, and the second Helvetic Confession. The language of the Belgic Confession, of date 1563, is not so guarded as that of those to which we have referred; but while it speaks of the natural body of Christ being eaten, it at the same time carefully excludes everything that would favour the theory of oral manducation, and expressly states that the manner of eating is not by the mouth of the body, but by the Spirit through faith.

It has been alleged by some that the doctrine taught in the Gallican Confession, in regard to the Sacrament of the Supper, does not harmonise with that laid down in the Confessions of the other Reformed Churches, inasmuch as the 36th article of said Confession favours the doctrine of the *local presence* of the body and blood of Christ in the Supper, and declares that we are nourished with the *substance* of Christ's body and blood. No doubt there is some ground for the allegation to which we have referred; but, when taken in connection with the explanation given of the article by the Synod of France to the Swiss Churches thirteen years after, it is clear that no such doctrine was held, or intended to be taught by them. It may therefore truly be affirmed that the doctrine taught by the Reformed Churches of England, Scotland, and the Continent, in regard to the sacraments, differs essentially from that of the Church of Rome, the Greek Church, the Lutheran

Church, the Scottish Communion Office, and the English Tractarians.

We come now to refer to the steps taken in the reign of Edward VI. by the King and Council, to take down any *altars* still remaining in any of the churches of the realm, and to "place *communion tables* in their stead," with the reasons assigned for so doing. The following is the letter of the Council "*to Bishop Ridley to take down altars, and place communion tables in their stead.*"

"Right reverend father in God, right trusty and well-beloved, we greet you well. And where it is come to our knowledge that, being the altars within the more part of the churches of this realm already upon good and godly considerations taken down, there doth yet remain altars standing in divers others churches, by occasion whereof much variance and contention ariseth among sundry of our subjects, which, if good foresight were not had, might perchance engender great hurt and inconvenience; we let you wit, that minding to have all occasion of contention taken away, which many times groweth by those and such like diversities, and considering that, amongst other things belonging to our royal office and cure, we do account the greatest to be, to maintain the common quiet of our realm; we have thought good by the advice of our council to require you, and nevertheless specially to charge and commend you, for the avoiding of all matters of further contention and strife about the standing or taking away of the said altars, to give substantial order throughout all your diocese, that with all diligence all the altars in every church or chapel, as well in places exempted, as not exempted, within your said diocese, be taken down, and in the stead of them a table to be set up in some convenient part of the chancel, within every such church or chapel, to serve for the ministration of the blessed communion. And to the intent the same may be done without the offence of such our loving subjects as be not yet so well persuaded in that behalf as we would wish, we send unto you herewith certain considerations gathered and collected, that make for the purpose; the which, and such other as you shall think meet to be set forth to persuade the weak to embrace our proceedings on this part, we pray you cause to be declared to the people by some discreet preachers, in such places as you shall think meet, before the taking down of the said altars; so as both the weak consciences of others may be instructed and satisfied as much as may be, and this our pleasure the more quietly executed. For the better doing whereof, we require you to open the foresaid considerations in that our cathedral church in your own person, if you conveniently may, or otherwise by your chancellor, or some other grave preacher, both there and in such other market towns and most notable places of your diocese, as you may judge most requisite.

"*Given under our signet, at our palace of Westminster, the 24th day of November, the fourth year of our reign.*"

The following are "the considerations" referred

to by the Council in their letter to Bishop Ridley:—

"*Reasons why the Lord's Board should rather be after the form of a Table than of an Altar.*

THE FIRST REASON.

"First, The form of a table shall more move the simple from the superstitious opinions of the Popish mass unto the right use of the Lord's Supper. For the use of an altar is to make sacrifice upon it; the use of a table is to serve for men to eat upon. Now, when we come unto the Lord's board, what do we come for? To sacrifice Christ again, and to crucify Him again; or to feed upon Him who was once only crucified and offered up for us? If we come to feed upon Him, spiritually to eat His body, and spiritually to drink His blood, which is the true use of the Lord's Supper, then no man can deny but the form of a table is more meet for the Lord's board than the form of an altar.

THE SECOND REASON.

"*Item*, Whereas it is said the Book of Common Prayer maketh mention of an altar, wherefore it is not lawful to abolish that which that book alloweth; to this it is thus answered: The Book of Common Prayer calleth the thing whereupon the Lord's Supper is ministered, indifferently a table, an altar, or the Lord's board, without prescription of any form thereof, either of a table or of an altar, so that whether the Lord's board have the form of an altar, or of a table, the Book of Common Prayer calleth it both an altar and a table. For, as it calleth it an altar, whereupon the Lord's Supper is ministered, a table, and the Lord's board; so it calleth the table where the Holy Communion is distributed, with lauds and thanksgiving unto the Lord, an altar; for that there is offered the same sacrifice of praise and thanksgiving. And thus it appeareth that here is nothing either said or meant contrary to the Book of Common Prayer.

THE THIRD REASON.

"Thirdly, The Popish opinion of mass was, that it might not be celebrated but upon an altar, or at the least upon a super-altar, to supply the fault of the altar, which must have had his prints and characters; or else it was thought that the thing was not lawfully done. But this superstitious opinion is more holden in the minds of the simple and ignorant by the form of an altar than of a table; wherefore it is more meet, for the abolishment of this superstitious opinion, to have the Lord's board after the form of a table than of an altar.

THE FOURTH REASON.

"Fourthly, The form of an altar was ordained for the sacrifices of the law, and therefore the altar in Greek is called θυσιαστηριον, *quasi sacrificii locus*. But now both the law and the sacrifices thereof do cease: wherefore the form of the altar used in the law ought to cease withal.

THE FIFTH REASON.

"Fifthly, Christ did institute the sacrament of His body and blood at His last supper at a table, and not at an altar, as it appeareth manifestly by the three Evangelists. And Saint Paul calleth the coming to the Holy Communion, the coming unto the Lord's Supper. And also it is not read that any of the Apostles, or the Primitive Church, did ever use any altar in ministration of the Holy Communion.

"Wherefore, seeing the form of a table is more agreeable with Christ's institution, and with the usage of the Apostles and of the Primitive Church, than the form of an altar, therefore the form of a table is rather to be used than the form of an altar in the administration of the Holy Communion.

THE SIXTH REASON.

"Finally, It is said, in the preface of the Book of Common Prayer, that if any doubt do arise in the use and practising of the same book; to appease all such diversity, the matter shall be referred unto the Bishop of the diocese, who by his discretion shall take order for the quieting and appeasing of the same, so that the same order be not contrary unto anything contained in that book."

Would that some one were to arise now in the Church of England, animated by the spirit of her early Reformers, to sweep away the mass of ritualistic rubbish which has been accumulating during the last quarter of a century!

THE DOCTRINE OF THE SACRAMENTS.

The doctrines which Cranmer, Ridley, and Latimer taught from the pulpit, and through the press, they afterwards sealed with their blood. "As concerning the sacrament," said Cranmer, when on his trial with a view to his condemnation, "I have taught no false doctrine respecting the sacrament of the altar; for if it can be proved by any doctor within a thousand years after Christ, that Christ's body is there really present, I will give over. My book was written seven years ago, and no man hath brought any authors against it." Ridley and Latimer were both charged, in the articles of impeachment drawn up against them, with affirming, and openly maintaining "that the true and natural body of Christ, after the consecration of the Priest, is not really present in the sacrament of the altar," and "that in the mass is no propitiatory sacrifice for the quick and the dead." And for maintaining these doctrines they were condemned as heretics, adjudged to be degraded from all ecclesiastical orders, declared to be no members of the Church, and "committed to the secular power to receive due punishment according to the temporal laws." They were both condemned to be burned, and when the fire was kindled, Latimer addressed these memorable words to his brother-martyr, "Be of good comfort, brother Ridley, and play the man; we shall this day light such a candle, by God's grace, in England, as I trust shall never be put out."

Not a few in the Church of England are now exerting themselves to the utmost of their power, to put out, if possible, the candle lighted by these illustrious martyrs. The doctrines proclaimed by Latimer and Ridley are irreconcilably opposed to those taught by Dr Pusey, Archdeacon Denison, and the ritualistic party. Notwithstanding of slight differences among themselves, in the way of defining the "real presence" for which they contend, they all agree in viewing it as an objective presence, as something united to, or in, with, or under, or conveyed by the consecrated elements. Nor does it mend the matter to call it "a spiritual presence;" on the contrary, it only tends to mystify and mislead, inasmuch as, by spiritual presence, they still mean an objective presence—viz., *the body of Christ present after the manner of a Spirit*, which is a contradiction in terms, and differs in no material respect from the doctrine of the Church of Rome as expounded and defended by Cardinal Bellarmine.

In His discourse in the synagogue at Capernaum —although not delivered in connection with the Sacrament of the Supper which had not then been instituted—our Lord proclaimed truths which are well fitted to guard us against gross or carnal views regarding that ordinance; for, while insisting on the necessity of eating His flesh and drinking His blood, He explains what is meant by so doing when He says, "He that believeth in me shall never thirst." And, again, in the 62d verse, "Doth this offend you? What, and if ye shall see the Son of man ascend where he was before?" As if He had said, Do not imagine that it is a carnal eating and drinking to which I am referring, that my flesh must be locally present, that it may be orally partaken of. No. The Son of man must soon ascend up where He was before. It is not His *bodily*, but His *spiritual* presence of which I am speaking. *It is the Spirit that quickeneth, the flesh profiteth nothing. The words that I speak unto you, they are spirit, and they are life.* Here our Lord distinctly affirms, and clearly teaches, if they had but spiritual apprehension to understand Him, that it was not by local presence, or carnal contact, but by His doctrine—His Word—carried home to their hearts and consciences, with quickening power, by the Spirit, that they were to feed upon Him—the bread of life, so as that they should never perish. When our Lord says, *He that believeth in me shall never* thirst, He plainly teaches that the eating and drinking of which He was speaking, were just figurative expressions for faith. And this is the doctrine which has been taught by the Church of Christ from the earliest ages. Hence says Athanasius, one of the greatest defenders of the Church, in primitive times, in his commentary upon this chapter: "To how many men would His body be sufficient for meat, that this should be the food of the whole world? Therefore He made mention of the ascension of the Son of man into heaven, that He might withdraw them from the contemplation of the body, and that they might learn that the flesh of which He spoke was heavenly food from above, and spiritual nourishment given by Him." And the greatest father of the early Church—Augustine—thus speaks, "Therefore the Lord being about to give the Holy Spirit called Himself the bread which came down from heaven, exhorting us to believe in Him. For to believe in Him, this is to eat the living bread. *He who believes, eats it.* What is bread from the kingdom of God, but He who says, 'I am the living bread which came down from heaven:' *Prepare not your mouth, but your heart; believe, and thou hast eaten.*" And to show the more clearly and conclusively that this eating is an act of the soul, not of the mouth—that it is nothing more nor less than faith in Christ, drawing spiritual nourishment from the living Saviour, and the truths which He taught—Augustine refers to the fact that the Old Testament saints thus fed upon Christ before His appearance in the flesh, "For they did all eat the same spiritual meat, and they did all drink the same spiritual drink, for they drank of that spiritual Rock that followed them, and that Rock was Christ." It is of importance to remember that eating and drinking are just significant figurative expressions *for faith*,—for the act of faith by which the soul feeds on a spiritually present, though bodily absent Saviour. This is all the more necessary as a spirit of sacerdotalism, or priestly carnalism, is extensively prevalent, which would transform the Lord's Table into an Altar, His ministering servants into sacrificing Priests, through whose acts the Body of Christ becomes in some mysterious manner objectively present in, with, or under the forms of bread and wine, being "localised in the consecrated elements," in some miraculous way transcending our comprehension, and is, therefore, literally partaken of, thus limiting the eating of the flesh of Christ, and the drinking of His blood, to a participation of them actually present in the ordinance of the Supper. And it is a remarkable circumstance that these views should now prevail, to a large extent, in that Church whose communion service is about the simplest of all the Churches of the Reformation; and which, as if anticipating the false doctrine above referred to, expressly guards her members against the carnal views embodied in it.

In the communion service of the Church of England for the sick, we have the following *injunction* and *instruction* to the minister, "But if a man, either by reason of extremity of sickness, or by any other just impediment, do not receive the sacrament of Christ's body and blood, the curate shall instruct him, that, if he do truly repent him of his sins, and steadfastly believe that Jesus Christ suffered upon the cross for him, and shed His blood for his redemption, earnestly remembering the benefits he hath thereby, and giving Him hearty thanks therefor, *he doth eat and drink the body and blood of our Saviour Christ, profitably to his soul's health, although he do not receive the sacrament with his mouth.*"

Thus the Church of England expressly declares that to believe in Christ, is to feed upon Him,—is to eat His flesh, and to drink His blood; thus clearly teaching that it is a spiritual act—an act of the soul—an act of faith, not of sense.

Thus, whether Christ is fed upon, in the ordinance of the Supper, or, apart from that ordinance, by the reading or preaching of the Word, *Faith* is the instrument by which, in either case, spiritual nourishment is drawn from Him. Hence the exhortation of Augustine already quoted, "*Prepare not your mouth, but your heart;* BELIEVE AND THOU HAST EATEN,"—an exhortation altogether irreconcilable with the theory of an objective presence in the Supper—a presence "localised in the consecrated elements," altogether irrespective and independent of the state of mind of the recipient.

CHAPTER VIII.

ON APOSTOLICAL SUCCESSION.

No evidence in support of it from the Scriptures—Condemned by the most eminent of the early Fathers, and the most learned Divines of the Church of England,—1. Irenæus, Tertullian, Cyprian, Ambrose, Gregory Nazianzen, Ambrose, Augustine, Jerome. 2. Bradford, Jewel, Hoadly, Whitaker, Field, Stillingfleet, Whately, Goode.

IN the "introduction" to the *Code of Canons* of the Scotch Episcopal Church, the members of the General Synod, of date 1863, make the following statement:—"The preservation of the Church's spiritual powers in the way of episcopal succession has ever marked the 'continuance' of Christians after the example of the early converts 'in the Apostles' doctrine and fellowship;' and from the constant attention shown to this ecclesiastical arrangement in the apostolic age, we may justly infer that it was then considered as one of those things which our Lord's Apostles were commanded to teach the nations to 'observe,' to watch over, and preserve in its pure and original form. Such is the form in which has been regularly handed down the ecclesiastical authority of the Episcopal Church in Scotland." (Introduction, p. v.)

The doctrine of apostolical succession is thus stated by Dr Hook in his *Two Sermons* on the Church and the Establishment : " The prelates who, at this present time, rule the churches of these realms, were validly ordained by others, who by means of an unbroken spiritual descent of ordination derived their mission from the Apostles, and from our Lord. This continual descent is evident to every one who chooses to investigate it. . . . . . There is not a Bishop, Priest, or Deacon among us who cannot, if he please, *trace his own spiritual descent* from St Peter or St Paul."

What this theory, then, asserts is, " that there has been a lineal, personal succession of validly consecrated prelates, without which there can be now no valid or proper ministerial succession at all ;"[*] and, consequently, no valid dispensation of ordinances or sacraments.

It has been shown, in previous chapters, that there is no evidence from the Scriptures, from the early Fathers, or the English Reformers, in support of the allegation that diocesan Bishops are an order superior to Presbyters, *de jure divino*.

We now affirm that there is no reliable evidence from any of these sources in support of the theory of apostolic succession.

[*] Smyth, p. 23.

ON APOSTOLICAL SUCCESSION. 105

The apostleship was an extraordinary office suited to the exigencies of an extraordinary time. The Apostles had peculiar and formidable difficulties to contend with. The old dispensation was passing away, but the Jews were nevertheless firmly wedded to it, were determined to hold by it, and so far from being favourably disposed to the gospel dispensation, which was to supersede it, scouted its claims; and crucified the Messiah, its Author and Founder, as a malefactor and deceiver; so that, in proclaiming the gospel among the Jews, the Apostles had to contend with peculiar, and, humanly speaking, insuperable difficulties. And if difficulties existed as respects the Jews, they also existed as respects the Gentiles. They were in spiritual darkness, and preferred the speculations of their own philosophers, and the reveries of science, falsely so called, to the sublime revelations of the Godhead. The peculiar doctrines of Christianity were most distasteful to them. Salvation through a crucified Redeemer was an offence to them, while the resurrection of the body appeared to them to be absurd and impossible. Now, in these circumstances, surrounded by peculiar difficulties, both as respects Jews and Gentiles, it is obvious that powers of no ordinary nature behoved to be conferred upon those sent forth to establish the new dispensation,—powers which would enable them to triumph over these apparently insurmountable obstacles, powers necessary to the founding and setting up of the New Testament Church in the critical and peculiar circumstances of the Church and of the world at the time; but powers which would be no longer necessary, *in the case of ordinary ministers,* when once the Church was established, and extended, settled, and put in order. And hence we find, in reading the inspired narrative, which gives an account of the founding and setting up of the New Testament Church, that extraordinary powers were conferred, that special and peculiar gifts were bestowed, and a class of extraordinary officers commissioned, and sent forth, —men who had the power of discerning spirits, who had the gift of prophecy, and could foretell future events, who had the power of working miracles, the gift of healing, and the gift of tongues; who were enabled to speak in languages which they had never learned, and thus go forth at once to preach the gospel to men of all kindreds, and tribes, and tongues. It was necessary that those invested with the apostleship should have seen the Lord, in order that thus they might be witnesses to the fact of His resurrection. And hence, in the election of a successor to Judas, the Church was restricted within the following limits, viz., they were to make choice of one who had companied with the Apostles all the time that the Lord went in and out among them, beginning from the baptism of John unto that same day that the Lord was taken up from them, that thus he might be a witness with them of His resurrection.*

The Apostles had seen the Lord, and had received

* Acts i. 21, 22.

their commission directly and personally at His hands. This qualification appears to have been absolutely necessary, and hence, when a doubt was raised as to the validity of the Apostle Paul's commission as an Apostle,* he sets himself to prove that he possessed all the necessary qualifications; that he had seen the Lord Jesus, for He had appeared to him, and gave him his commission; and he appeals to the Corinthians that he had also wrought among them the signs of an Apostle. The Apostleship, then, in its leading, distinguishing features, was an extraordinary office suited to the exigencies of an extraordinary time; and just as the office of Prophet, as far as the receiving of revelations of things future is concerned, ceased when John received the last message in Patmos, so the office of Apostle, in the distinctive sense of the term, ceased when the New Testament dispensation was established. And hence we find no men now who possess either the qualifications or the powers of Apostles, strictly so called—no men who have seen the Lord, and received their commission, not mediately through the hands of men, but directly from the Great Head of the Church Himself—no men who possess the gift of tongues, and the power of working miracles. In all these peculiarities of the Apostleship, the Apostles have no successors. The only part of their office in which they have successors is in the Presbyterate, or Eldership,—in other words, in preaching the gospel, and administering ordinances.

* 1 Cor. ix. 1; xv. 7, 8, 9; 2 Cor. xi. 5; xii. 12.

And they only are the successors of the Apostles, in that part of their office which remains, who preach that doctrine which they preached, unmutilated and unaltered; who proclaim that gospel which they proclaimed, and point to that Saviour to whom they pointed. The only succession worth the having is not through Popes and Prelates,—not through a mass of spurious parchments, and moral corruption, but a succession of apostolic *spirit*, of apostolic *doctrine*, and apostolic *practice*.

"Successors," says Archbishop Whately, in his "Kingdom of Christ," "in the apostolic office, the Apostles have none. As *witnesses of the resurrection*, as *dispensers* of *miraculous* gifts, as inspired oracles of divine revelation, they have no successors. But as *members*, as *ministers*, as governors of Christian communities, their successors are the regularly admitted members, the lawfully ordained ministers, the regular and recognised governors of a regularly subsisting Christian Church."

In short, in the words of Dodwell, one of the most learned defenders of Episcopacy which the Church of England has ever possessed,—" The office of the Apostles *perished with the Apostles*, in which office *there never was any succession to any of them, except to Judas the traitor.*" Dodwell might safely have added that a long and infamous catalogue of Popes and Prelates, exemplifying the *latter line of succession*, could easily be furnished.

Let us now inquire whether this doctrine of the necessity of an unbroken line of office-bearers, by episcopal prelatic descent from the Apostles, in order to the valid dispensation of Word and Sacraments, was held by the early Fathers.

It has been conclusively demonstrated not only by Presbyterians, but also by able and learned Episcopal divines, such as Stillingfleet, and the late Dean of Ripon, Dr Goode, by evidence which never has been, and never can be met, that, so far from holding or countenancing the doctrine in question, the early Fathers put upon it the stamp of their reprobation, and teach that the true test by which to try, and the true method by which to establish a claim to descent from the Apostles, is not by a mere succession of persons, but a succession and exhibition of *apostolic doctrine.* The following are the testimonies on this point of Irenæus, Tertullian, Gregory of Nazianzen, Ambrose, Cyprian, and Augustine.

1. Irenæus:—In warning those to whom he wrote against heretics, Irenæus refers to two different kinds of *succession*,—a *succession* represented by those who had received "the sure gift of truth," and another represented by those "who are looked upon by many as Presbyters, but serve their own pleasures, and do not in their hearts make the fear of God their rule, but persecute others with reproaches, and are elated with pride AT THEIR EXALTATION TO THE CHIEF SEAT, and secretly do evil and say, 'No one seeth us.' They shall be reproved by the Word, who does not judge after outward appearance, nor looks upon the countenance, but the heart.

.... From all such persons it behoves us to stand aloof, but to adhere to those who, as I have already observed, do hold the DOCTRINE of the Apostles, and who, together with the order of the Presbytership (*Presbyterii ordine*), display sound speech, and a blameless conversation, for the edification and correction of the rest." *

The succession of which Irenaeus speaks is a succession of *Presbyters*, (of parochial Bishops, not of Prelates); of Presbyters who, along with the succession of the Episcopate, have received, according to the good pleasure of the Father, the sure gift of truth—qui cum episcopatus successione charisma veritatis certum secundum placitum Patris acceperunt.

Now, it is one thing to speak of a succession of *Presbyters*, or Congregational Bishops, and another to admit a succession of *Prelates*. To admit the former is only saying in other words that God has never been without His witnesses; that in every age of the Church he has had His faithful ministers. But while that is unquestionably true, it is equally true that the real and only test by which to try the spirits whether they be of God is not an unbroken chain either of Presbyters or of Prelates, every link in which must, without fail, be visibly traced up to the Apostles, or any other conceivable succession of *persons* but that which is referred to by Irenaeus, viz., a succession of *apostolic doctrine*, of the *sure gift of truth* received from the Father.

* Iren. Adv. hær. lib. iv. c. 26.

2. Tertullian :—" Nay, even if they should do so, they will have done nothing. For their doctrine, when compared with the apostolical, will show, from its difference and contrariety, that it has neither an Apostle nor a disciple of the Apostles for its author; for, as the Apostles would not have differed from one another in their teaching, so neither would the disciples of the Apostles have preached a different doctrine from that of the Apostles, unless those who were taught by the Apostles preached otherwise than they were taught. By this test, therefore, they shall be tried by those churches which, although they can produce no Apostle or disciple of the Apostles as their author, as being of much later origin, and such indeed are daily formed, yet, agreeing in the same faith, are considered as not less apostolical on account of the consanguinity of their doctrine." *

3. Ambrose :—" If there is any Church," says Ambrose, " which rejects the faith, and does not possess the fundamentals of the doctrine of the Apostles, it is to be deserted." † And elsewhere, " They have not the inheritance, are not the successors of Peter, who have not Peter's faith."

4. Gregory of Nazianzen :—" If you consider Athanasius only as one of the number of Bishops of Alexandria, he was the most remote from St Mark; but if you regard his piety, you find him

---

* De Praescript, c. 32.
† Ambros. in Luc. lib. vi., s. 68, (quoted in Goode's Rule of Faith, vol. ii., p. 341.)

the very next to him. This succession of piety ought to be esteemed the true succession. For he who maintains the same doctrine of faith, is partner in the same chair; but he who defends a contrary doctrine ought, though in the chair of St Mark, to be esteemed an adversary to it. This man, indeed, may have a *nominal* succession, but the other has the *very thing itself, the succession in deed and in truth.*

Or more concisely, and literally, "For to *hold the same doctrine*, is to be of *the same throne;* but to hold an *opposite doctrine*, is to be of an opposite throne." (Τὸ μὲν γὰρ ὁμόγνωμον καὶ ὁμόθρονον· τὸ δὲ ἀντίδοξον καὶ ἀντίθρονον.) "Neither," he continues, "is he who usurps the chair by violent means to be esteemed in the succession, but he who is pressed into the office; not he who violates all law in his election, but he who is elected in a manner consistent with the laws of the case; not he who holds doctrines opposed to what St Mark taught, but he who is endued with the same faith as St Mark. Except, indeed, you intend to maintain such a succession as that of sickness succeeding to health, light succeeding to darkness, a storm to a calm, and madness succeeding to soundness of mind! It was not with Athanasius as it is sometimes with tyrants, who, being suddenly raised to the throne, break out into acts of violence and excess. Such conduct as this is the mark of adulterate and spurious Bishops, and who are unworthy of the dignity to which they are raised.

These having no previous qualifications for their office, never having borne the trials of virtue, commence disciples and masters at the same time, and attempt to consecrate others whilst unholy themselves. Yesterday they were guilty of sacrilege, to-day they are made ministers of the sanctuary; yesterday they were ungodly, to-day they are made reverend fathers in God; old in sin, ignorant of piety, and having proceeded in violence in all the rest, (as not being influenced by divine but human motives,) they crown the whole by exercising their tyranny upon piety itself.*

5. Cyprian :—" What," asks Cyprian, when opposing Stephen, Bishop of Rome, "does he mean by tradition? Does he mean the authority of Christ in the gospels, and of the Apostles in their epistles? Let this tradition be sacred; for if we return to this head and original of divine tradition, human error will cease. If the channel of the water of life, at first coming down in large and copious flow, should suddenly fail, should we not return to the *fountain.* This ought the ministers of God now to do, observing, *as their rule*, the divine precepts, that if anything has tottered and shaken from the truth, it should be restored to the authority of Christ, the Evangelists, and the Apostles, and all our proceedings are to take their rise there, whence all order and divine authority rise, *for custom without truth is only antiquated error.* Therefore, forsaking

---

* Athanasii Opp., vol. ii., Appendix, Edit. Paris, 1627. Orat. in Athanas., vol. i., p. xciii., E. Benedictine Edition.

error, let us follow the truth. Truth lives and reigns through endless ages. Neither is there with truth any distinction or respect of persons, but only that which is just it ratifies; neither is there in the jurisdiction of truth any iniquity, but the strength and dominion, and the majesty and power of all generations. Blessed be the God of truth! This truth Christ shows in the gospel, saying, 'I am the truth.' Therefore, if we be in Christ, and Christ in us; if we remain in the truth, and the truth abide in us, let us hold those things which are of the truth."*

6. Augustine:—"We ought to find the Church, as the Head of the Church, in the Holy Canonical Scriptures, not to inquire for it in the various reports, and opinions, and deeds, and visions of men." Again, "Whether they (*i.e.*, the Donatists), hold the Church, they must show by the Canonical books of the Divine Scriptures alone; for we do not say, that we must be believed because we are in the Church of Christ, because Optatus of Milevi, or Ambrose of Milan, or innumerable other Bishops of our communion, commended that Church to which we belong, or because it is extolled by the Councils of our colleagues, or because through the whole world, in the holy places which those of our communion frequent, such wonderful answers to prayer, or cures happen. . . . Wherever things of this kind take place in the Catholic Church, are therefore to be approved of because they take place

* Epist. 74, edit. Parnel., 1589.

in the Catholic Church; but it is not proved to be the Catholic Church, because these things happen in it. The Lord Jesus Himself, when He had risen from the dead, . . . judged that His disciples were to be convinced by the testimonies of *the Law and the Prophets and the Psalms.* . . . *These are the proofs, these the foundations, these the supports of our cause.* We read in the Acts of the Apostles of some who believed, that they searched the Scriptures daily, whether those things were so. What Scriptures but the Canonical Scriptures of the Law and the Prophets? To these have been added the Gospels, the Apostolical Epistles, the Acts of the Apostles, the Apocalypse of John."*

Having thus seen that the doctrine in question, as held by modern High Churchmen, received no countenance from the fathers of the early Church; let us now inquire what were the views entertained on the subject by the early fathers of the Church of England. A long list of testimonies by learned and distinguished men might easily be produced,— as Bradford, Jewell, Hall, Whitaker, Hoadly, Field, Stillingfleet, &c., &c.

First, we shall give the judgment of John Bradford, who was burned at Smithfield, in the reign of Mary. In his examination before Bishops Gardiner, and Bonner, Archdeacon Harpsfield having brought forward the doctrine of the succession of Bishops, as an essential and testing point, Bradford replied,

---

* August. Contr. Donat. Ep. (vulg. De unitate eccles.) c. 19. Op. tom. ix. col. 372, 73.

"You say as you would have it; for if this point fail you, all the Church that you go about to set up will fall down. You will not find in all the Scripture this your *essential point of the succession of Bishops*. In Christ's Church Antichrist will sit:— The ministry of God's Word and ministers be an essential point. But to translate this to the Bishops and their succession, is a plain subtilty. And therefore that it may be plain, I will ask you a question,—Tell me, whether that the Scripture knew any difference between Bishops and ministers, which ye call priests, (Presbyters)? Harpsfield: No. Bradford: Well, then, go on forward and let us see what ye will get now by the succession of Bishops; that is, of ministers, which can be understood of such Bishops as minister not, but lord it. Harpsfield: I perceive that ye are far out of the way. Bradford: If Christ or His Apostles being here on earth had been required by the Prelates of the Church then, to have made a demonstration of that Church by succession of such High Priests as had approved the doctrines which He taught, I think Christ would have done as I do, that is, (He would) have alleged that which upholdeth the Church, even the verity, the Word of God taught and believed, not by the High Priests which of long time had persecuted it, but by the Prophets and other good simple men, which perchance were counted for heretics of the Church, which Church was not tied to succession, but to the Word of God."*

* Fox's Acts, &c., vol. iii., p. 293, &c. Ed. 1641.

"The true visible Church," says White, Bishop of Ely, "is named Apostolical, not because of local and personal succession of Bishops, (only or principally), but because it retaineth the FAITH and DOCTRINE of the Apostles. Personal, or local succession only, and in itself, maketh not the Church Apostolical, because hirelings and wolves may lineally succeed lawful and orthodox pastors, (Acts xx. 29, 30,) *even as sickness succeedeth health, and darkness light, and a tempest fair weather*, as Gregory Nazianzen affirmeth.*

"For that ye tell so many fair tales about Peter's succession, we demand of you, (says Bishop Jewel), wherein the Pope succedeth Peter? You answer, he succeeded him in his chair; as if Peter had been some time installed in Rome, and had solemnly sat all day with his triple crown, in his *Pontificalibus*, and in a chair of gold. And thus, having lost both RELIGION and DOCTRINE, you think it sufficient, at last, to hold by the *chair*, as if a soldier that had lost his sword, would play the man with his scabbard. But so Caiaphas succeeded Aaron; so wicked Manasses succeeded David; so may ANTICHRIST easily sit in *Peter's Chair*."†

"TRUTH OF DOCTRINE," says Field, "is a necessary note whereby the Church must be known and discerned, and *not ministry or succession, or anything else*, without it." ‡

---

* Bishop White's Works, p. 64. Ed. 1624.
† Defence of Apol. Ed. 1609, p. 634.
‡ Field on the Church. Book ii. c. 6.

In demonstrating the irrelevancy of Bellarmine's argument, founded upon the testimonies of the early Fathers, Whitaker says, "This argument proves not that the succession of persons alone is conclusive, or sufficient of itself; but only that it avails when they had *first proved* (*from the Scriptures*) that the faith they preached was the same faith which the Apostles had preached before them. *Faith*, therefore, is as it were the *soul* of the succession; which faith being wanting, the naked succession of persons is like a DEAD CARCASE WITHOUT THE SOUL." *

"I am fully satisfied," says Bishop Hoadly, "that till a consummate stupidity can be happily established, and universally spread over the land, there is nothing that tends so much to destroy all due respect to the clergy, as the demand of more than can be due to them; and nothing has so effectually thrown contempt upon a regular succession of the ministry, as the calling *no succession regular*, *but what was uninterrupted*; and the making the eternal salvation of Christians to depend upon that uninterrupted succession, of which *the most learned* must have *the least assurance*, and the unlearned can have no notice, but through ignorance and credulity." †

"*If they preach Christ*," says Bishop Hall, "they are Pastors and Doctors allowed by Christ. We stand not upon circumstances and appendances of

---

* Whitaker's Works, vol. i., p. 506. Ed. Genev. 1610.
† Buck's Theol. Dict., Art. Succession.

the fashions of ordination, manner of choice, attire, TITLES, maintenance; but, if for substance these, (viz., *they who preach Christ*) be not true Pastors and Doctors, Christ *had never* any in His Church since the Apostles left the earth." *

The last testimony which I shall cite from Church of England Divines is that of Stillingfleet. "What becomes, then," he asks, "of our unquestionable line of succession of the Bishops of several Churches, and the large diagrams made of the Apostolical Churches with every one's name set down in his order, as if the writer had been *Clarenceaulx* to the Apostles themselves? Is it come to this at last that we have nothing certain but what we have in the Scriptures? and must then the tradition of the Church be our rule to interpret Scripture by? An excellent way to find out the truth, doubtless, to bend the rule to the crooked stick, to make the judge stand to the opinion of his lacquey, what sentence we shall pass upon the cause in question; to make Scripture stand cap in hand to tradition to know whether it may have leave to speak or no. Are all the great outcries of Apostolical tradition, of personal succession, of unquestionable records, resolved at last into the Scripture itself by him (Eusebius) from whom all these wrong pedigrees are fetched."

The probability against such a pedigree being established is well-nigh infinite. The very first link in the chain is doubtful. There is no reliable evi-

* Hall's Apol. against Brownists, p. 31.

dence to show that Peter ever was at Rome; or, granting that he had been at Rome, and had a successor, no evidence to show who that successor was.

In regard to this latter point, the early Fathers and divines of the Church of England are hopelessly divided among themselves.

The chain is purely an inductive one, and therefore one flaw would prove fatal to the validity of the whole. It is a chain from which

"Whichever link you strike
Tenth or ten-thousandth breaks the chain alike."

Stillingfleet shows that the boasted line of succession is defective, ambiguous, partial, and confused; that as respects Jerusalem and Antioch, it is far from clear; as regards Rome, that it is *muddy as the Tiber*; and that, as regards Alexandria, where it is clearest, and seems most free from doubt, the succession is PRESBYTERIAL.

Eusebius, who attempted, at an early period, to trace the line of succession, and who is a great authority with High Churchmen, tells us that, in doing so, he had "to tread a solitary and untrodden way, and could nowhere find footsteps of any who had passed before;" and speaking of *Paul* and *Peter*, and the Churches planted by them, he confesses that, as to their successors, it is hard to find out who they were, unless those mentioned by Paul himself in his epistles, thus bringing us back to the Scriptures as the only reliable source of information on the subject.*

* Eusebius, Hist. Eccl., lib. iii., c. 4.

To attempt to trace the line of succession " is to follow the scent of the game into the wood of antiquity, where it is easier to lose one's-self than to find that of which we are in pursuit."

What Stillingfleet says in regard to the want of reliable information as to many of the *places* in which the Apostles are said to have laboured, may also justly be said in reference to their successors,—instead of undoubted lists, " we have nothing but the forgeries of later ages to supply vacuity," furnished by "historical tinkers who think to mend a hole where they find it, and make three instead of it."*

As we come down the stream, the succession becomes *muddy* indeed. Common decency prevents us from describing such links in the chain as John X.; John XI.; Alexander VI., &c.

A darker portrait of many of those through whom the mysterious spiritual virtue is said to have descended cannot be drawn than that presented by Cardinal Baronius, the celebrated Roman Catholic historian, the Confessor of Clement VIII., the Curator of the Vatican Library, and the author of the "Annales Ecclesiastici," in twelve folio volumes. He tells us that Bishops were frequently elected by the influence of the most abandoned women of Rome; and that *false Popes, their paramours*, were thrust into the chair of Peter; and that these false Popes have a place in the CATALOGUES OF THE POPES OF ROME. The description, however, can be

* Irenicum, p. 296.

given with greater propriety under the veil of a dead language. It is thus given by Baronius himself:—
"*Quae tunc facies sanctae Ecclesiae Romanae! quàm faedissima cùm Romae dominarentur potentissimae aeque et sordidissimae meretrices! quarum arbitrio mutarentur sedes, darentur Episcopi, et quod auditu horrendum et infandum est, intruderentur in sedem Petri earum amassii Pseudo-Pontifices, que non sint nisi ad consignanda tantum tempora in catalogo Romanorum Pontificum Scripti. Quis enim à scortis hujusmodi intrusos sine lege legitimos dicere posset Romanos fuisse Pontifices?*"

As regards the Church of England, not a few of the links are of very doubtful canonical value. Plegmund, Archbishop of Canterbury, was ordained by Pope Formosus, all of whose ordinations were declared null and void by his successor Stephen VI., and also by Sergius III.

Chichley, also Archbishop of Canterbury, was ordained by Gregory XII. Now, Gregory was one of *three claimants* of the Popedom, and was afterwards deposed by the Council of Constance, and declared to be no POPE AT ALL, *but a mere pretender.* The ordinations of Bishops, by these two Archbishops, extend over half a century, certainly quite enough to vitiate the boasted line of succession, and to render it canonically worthless.

Even granting the validity and integrity of the chain of succession, it no more follows that prelatic Bishops are successors of the Apostles, *as such, or strictly so called,* than that the Marquis of Bute, in virtue of undoubted lineal descent from his ancestor, who was Premier in the reign of George III., is either, *de jure* or *de facto*, Prime Minister of Great Britain. The chain, however, is so far from being either valid or whole, that the late Archbishop Whately was not speaking without warrant when he affirmed "that there is not a minister *in all Christendom* who is able to trace up, with any approach to certainty, his own spiritual pedigree."

Parochial Bishops—that is, Presbyters—have existed in the Church of Christ in all ages; but, of prelatic or diocesan Bishops, the apostolic age, and that following, knew nothing.

For the faithful and zealous evangelical ministers of the Church of England we entertain great respect. We bid them God-speed in their labours. Would they were multiplied tenfold; but as respects the diocesan Bishops of that Church, however eminent many of them may be for piety, however earnest in work, and distinguished for learning, if their claim to rank as ministers of Christ, *is made to depend upon the figment of a pretentious lineal prelatic descent from the Apostles*, we have no hesitation in saying that, *as far as any such claim is concerned*, it must be said of them, as was said of the children of the priests, the children of Habaiah, the children of Koz, the children of Barzillai, "THESE SOUGHT THEIR REGISTER AMONG THOSE THAT WERE RECKONED BY GENEALOGY, BUT THEY WERE NOT FOUND : therefore were they, AS POLLUTED, PUT FROM THE PRIESTHOOD." (Ezra ii. 62.)

CHAPTER IX.

CONCLUSIONS ARRIVED AT.

Difference of Opinion among Episcopal Authors—Council of Trent—Provincial Assembly of London in 1653—Joannes Major—Fordon—Forbes—Bellarmine—Leighton's Zion's Plea against Prelacy.

THE ablest divines of the Church of England who have written on the subject of Church government, are far from being agreed among themselves. Some of them hold that the order of Bishop is superior to that of Presbyter, *jure apostolico*, but not *juris divini*; some, that it is superior *de jure positivo*, and others that it is superior, by a prudent arrangement of the magistrate for the sake of convenience and good order; while in the Council of Trent, where the subject was keenly debated, great diversity of opinion prevailed, — the Spaniards insisting that Bishops were superior to Presbyters *de jure divino*, and the Romish party holding, with Lanetius, General of the Jesuits, Prelates, *jure canonico*, to be merely from the Pope's authority.

The following conclusions, gathered from an examination of the ancient Romish, Greek, and African Churches, have been thus expressed by "The Provincial Assembly of London," in 1653 :—

"1. That there was a time when Presbyters did govern by common council, and did ordain without Bishops. So saith Panormitan, Olim Presbyteri in communi regebant Ecclesiam, et Ordinabant Sacredotes.

"2. That whole nations have been converted to the faith, and governed for hundreds of years without Bishops. This conclusion is abundantly proved by D. Blondel, sect. 3, de Ordinationibus, where he tells us that Joannes Major, de gestis Scotorum, lib. ii., cap. 2, saith, Per Sacerdotes, et Monachos sine Episcopis Scoti in fide eruditi: That Joannes Fordonius saith, Ante Palladii adventum, habebant Scoti fidei Doctores, ac Sacramentorum Ministratores Presbyteros solummodò vel Monachos, ritum sequentes Ecclesiæ Primitiva. The Scots were Christians two hundred and twenty years and more without Episcopal government. The like he proves of the Goths and French. For brevity sake, we refer the reader to the author himself.

"3. That in Egypt, when the Bishop was absent, Presbyters did consecrate.

"4. That in Alexandria, for about two hundred years, the Presbyters constituted and ordained their Bishop.

"5. That, though by the Canons of the Church the power of Presbyters in ordaining was restrained, yet it was the judgment of antiquity, that every Presbyter hath *actum primum*, and an inward power to ordain, and that, though his power was impedited by the Canons, yet it was not utterly extinguished.

"6. That when a Presbyter is made a Bishop, he hath no new power conferred upon him, but only his former restraints and impediments are removed, as saith Aureolus.

"7. That the Chorepiscopi for a certain space did ordain of their own authority, without receiving authority from the Bishop. Afterwards (though they were mere Presbyters), yet notwithstanding, by the leave of Councils, had liberty, with the Bishop's licence, to ordain.

"8. That to this day it is the opinion of Schoolmen and Canonists, that the Pope may give liberty to a Presbyter to ordain. From whence, saith Dr Forbes, it evidently followeth, Ordinationem quæ per solos Presbyteros peragitur non esse de jure divino invalidam neque Ordinationem esse de jure Divino ita propriam Episcoporum, ut non possit validè peragi per solos Presbyteros: That is, That ordination which is by Presbyters alone is not by divine right invalid, neither is ordination so proper by divine right to a Bishop, that it may not be done (even in the opinion of Papists themselves) by Presbyters alone. For otherwise the Pope could not commit ordination unto Presbyters. For Bellarmine saith expressly, In jure divino non potest Papa dispensare: The Pope cannot dispense in things that are by divine right. And Aureolus saith, Ea quæ sunt ordinum omnes recipiunt immediatè à Christo, ita quod in potestate nullius imò nec Papae est illa auferre; quæ sunt autem jurisdictionis, potest ea Papa suspendere. Now, then, from hence we may argue.

"That which by divine authority is to be done only by Bishops, that neither Bishops, nor Councils, nor Pope can commit to Presbyters that are not Bishops. Nam in jure divino Papa non potest dispensare. But (according to the judgment and practice of antiquity) the Pope may give the liberty and power of ordaining to Presbyters that are not Bishops; and Bishops also may do the like. Therefore the liberty and power of ordaining is not by divine right belonging to Bishops only, but may be lawfully done by others, the Papists themselves being judges."*

That Presbyters are an order in the Church, *de jure divino*, is admitted by Papists and Episcopalians; but that diocesan or prelatic Bishops are so, can never be proved from the Word of God. That they are of advantage, as a matter of prudential arrangement for the sake of government and good order, there is nothing in the history of the Church to prove. On the contrary, history furnishes ample evidence to show that the Church has no need of them whatever.

Dr Leighton, father of the Archbishop, puts this clearly and forcibly in his "Zion's Plea against Prelacy," and therefore with his summary we conclude.

* Jus Divinum Ministerii Anglicani, Ed. 1654, Appendix, pp. 140-42.

"Where the Spirit recounteth by name all the sorts of ministry, ordinary and extraordinary, of his own appointment (Eph. iv. 11), there is not one word of such a lording ministry, which the Spirit would not have concealed, but undoubtedly set them out with all their titles and prerogatives, if there had been any such superior offices of his appointment and approving. Is it a likely thing that God, who appointed the temple and the tabernacle, should be so punctual in every particular of His service under the law, and that He would conceal His more especial officers and their offices under the gospel? Would He remember the bars of the ark, and pass by the pillars of His Church? Would He appoint the least pins of the house, and forget the master builders? Would He there mention the snuffers of the lights, and here pass by the great lights themselves? Or, would He there remember the besoms and ashpans, and here not once mention Bishops and Archbishops? This were—τα μικρα οραν· και τα μεγαλα παρωραν—to look to small things, and overlook the great things. Is it true that a silly ignorant woman tells us in the gospel, that when the Messiah cometh He would tell us all things? (John iv. 25.) And yet He speaketh never one word of His special offices. Sure these cannot agree.

"From the same place of the Ephesians it will appear that such Bishops and their dependencies are superfluous, therefore they should have no place in God's house. The consequence is clear, because there is a necessary use of everything that hath any use in God's house.

"Nihil tam necessarium quàm cognoscere quid sibi sit necessarium—there is nothing so necessary, saith a father, as to know what is necessary or of use. Now that there is no use of them, it is cleared thus:—

"Those officers without which the Church of God is fully built up and brought to complete perfection of unity, are not of any use in God's house.

"But without the function of Lord Bishops, Archbishops, &c., the Church of God is fully built up and brought to complete perfection of unity, witness Eph. iv. 11-13.

"Therefore Lord Bishops, Archbishops, &c., are of no use in God's Church. The learned have used the same argument against the Pope, the Church of God being built up and perfected without him; therefore, he should not be. The argument is every way as good as against these Bishops and every such officer in God's house, without the which His house is complete, as against the Pope; for it cannot be said of those Bishops, as the Lord said of the ass, The Lord hath need of them, (Matt. xxi. 3.)"

CHAPTER X.

THE DOCTRINE OF THE ROYAL SUPREMACY, AND THE SPIRITUAL INDEPENDENCE OF THE CHURCH.

Debates in the Westminster Assembly— Coleman—Lightfoot, Selden, Gillespie—The Thirty-Seventh Article of the Church of England—The Injunctions of Queen Elizabeth—The Irish Articles—Latimer—Cranmer — Usher—John Livingstone—Alexander Henderson—Sir Roundell Palmer—Dr Ball.

> "The princes and powers of the world are more jealous than they need to be of the Church's strength; and yet (which is a secret judgment of God) they have not been afraid to suffer Babylon to be built in her full strength: 'There were they in great fear, where no fear was' (Ps. liii. 5); for when all shall come to all, it shall be found that the gospel and true religion is the strongest bulwark, and chief strength for the safety and stability of kings and states."—*Gillespie's Sermon before the House of Commons, of date March 27, 1644.*

ONE of the ablest treatises in defence of the spiritual freedom of the Church of Christ which the world has yet seen is the learned and valuable work on the Divine Right of Church Government, put forth by Ministers of the City of London, on the 1st December 1646, while the Westminster Assembly was yet sitting; a third edition of which, somewhat augmented, was called for in 1654.* The circumstances which called it forth were the struggles which were then being carried on between the Parliament of England and the Westminster Assembly in regard to the nature and limits of the power of the Civil Magistrate on the one hand, and the Church on the other; the Parliament insisting upon their right to an Erastian control over the Church, and the Assembly, while acknowledging the power of the Civil Magistrate to a certain extent *circa sacra*, nobly and resolutely refusing to acknowledge his right to any power or jurisdiction whatever *in sacris*. The determination of the Parliament to assume and exercise jurisdiction in spiritual matters came out very strongly on various occasions, and in divers manners; as, for instance, in the matter of suspension " of scandalous and ignorant persons " from the Sacrament of the Lord's Supper, in the matter of the Church's right to ordain ministers in the exercise of her own divinely-conferred powers, and in the matter of appeals, not from the *inferior ecclesiastical judicatories* to the higher, which the Church admitted and provided for, but *from the highest Ecclesiastical Court to the Paliament*, by whom, or by whose Commissioners, judgment was *finally* to be given. It is evident that the power thus claimed

* Jus Divinum Regiminis Ecclesiastici; or, the Divine Right of Church Government asserted and evidenced by the Holy Scriptures. By sundry Ministers of Christ within the City of London.

by the Parliament virtually obliterates all distinction between things civil and spiritual, as it practically hands over to the Civil Magistrate all authority and jurisdiction whether in things civil or ecclesiastical, temporal or spiritual, and is therefore absolutely incompatible with the proposition laid down by the Westminster Divines in Chapter xxx., Section 1, of the Confession of Faith. That proposition is as follows:—" The Lord Jesus, as King and Head of His Church, hath therein appointed a government in the hand of Church officers, distinct from the Civil Magistrate." This noble proposition, so clear and explicit in its terms—with the three subsequent sections relative to the power of the keys in the matter " of Church censures "—was the battle-field on which the Erastian controversy was mainly carried on in the Westminster Assembly.

As the principle upon which the Assembly proceeded was to ground all their propositions on the Word of God, and thus to fortify them by Divine authority, the Erastians, finding that it was impossible for them to attain their desired end unless they could successfully appeal to the same infallible standard, made a bold attempt to justify the controlling power which they claimed for the Civil Magistrate over the Church by a reference to 1 Cor. xii. 28—" And God hath set some in the Church, first, apostles; secondarily, prophets; thirdly, teachers; after that miracles; then gifts of healings, helps, *governments*, diversities of tongues." The term *governments*, in the foregoing passage, they contended had a reference to Christian Magistrates, who were thus, *jure divino*, in virtue of their office as Magistrates, rulers or governors in the Christian Church. This was the position taken up and contended for by Coleman and Lightfoot in the Assembly, and by the rector of Chesilhurst, Mr Hussey.

In his sermon before the House of Commons on the 30th of July 1645, Coleman says :—

3. "*Lay no more burden of government upon the shoulders of ministers than Christ hath plainly laid upon them.* The ministers have other work to do, and such as will take up the whole man, might I measure others by myself. It was the King of Sodom's speech to Abraham, 'Give me the persons; take thou the goods.' So say I, Give us doctrine; take you the government. As is said, Right Honourable, give me leave to make this request in the behalf of the ministry, Give us two things, and we shall do well—learning and a competency."

4. "*A Christian magistrate, as a Christian magistrate, is a governor in the Church.* Christ has placed government in His Church, (1 Cor. xii. 28.) Of other governments, beside magistracy, I find no institution; of them I do, (Rom. xii. 1, 2.) I find all government given to Christ, and to Christ as Mediator, (Eph. i. 22, 23.) I desire all to consider it. To rob the kingdom of Christ of the magistrate, and His governing power, I cannot excuse; no, not from a kind of sacrilege, if the magistrate be His."

As put by Hussey, the Erastian principle appears

in its most unqualified form, and may be summed up and expressed in the latter of the two following propositions :—

1. "All government is given to Christ *as Mediator*; and,

2. "Christ, *as Mediator*, has placed the Christian magistrate under Him, and as His vicegerent, and has given him commission to govern the Church."

The arguments advanced by Coleman in his sermon, and also by Hussey, as well as by Selden, the leader and champion of the Erastian party, were thoroughly demolished by Gillespie in his "Brotherly Examination" of said sermon—in his *Nihil Respondes*, being his reply to Coleman's attempted defence; in his *Male Audis;* and, more especially, in his immortal work—*Aaron's Rod Blossoming*, in which he demonstrates the untenableness of the views of Selden, Coleman, and Hussey, and which contains one of the most learned, conclusive, and exhaustive refutations of the Erastian theory which the world has ever seen.

In refuting the doctrine of the Erastians, Gillespie enters into an elaborate investigation into "the nature and extent of the Mediatorial sovereignty of Christ," distinguishing between His Headship over the Church, and his Kingly authority, as the eternal Son of God, over the nations, and clearly showing that the doctrine that the magistrate "holds his office *of*, under, and for Christ, *as He is Mediator*, and doth act *vice Christi*, as Christ's vicegerent," has no warrant whatever in the Word of God; while it is equally clear from the Word of God that magistracy, as well as all other things, has been put in subjection to Christ, and that the magistrate, as such, is to use his office and authority so as to be serviceable to Christ and His cause, and promotive of the interests of His Church in the world. "The distinction," says Gillespie, in concluding the argument in his *Male Audis*, "of the twofold kingdom of Christ—an universal kingdom, whereby He reigneth over all things as God, and a special economical kingdom, whereby He is King to the Church only, and ruleth and governeth it—is that which, being rightly understood, overturneth, overturneth, overturneth, the Erastian principles."

There are two primary principles, a right understanding of which is necessary in order to scriptural views on this important subject—First, The Headship of Christ over the Church; and second, His Kingly authority over the nations. 1. Christ is Head of the Church, which is His body—His mediatorial kingdom strictly and properly so called. From that great doctrine springs the spiritual independence of the Church—as respects the power conferred upon Church officers on the one hand, and the rights and liberties of the Christian people on the other. 2. Christ, as the eternal Son of God, is Prince of the kings of the earth, and Governor among the nations. He has, also, as the Lord's anointed, by express appointment and donation by the Father, had all things put under Him—nothing excepted, magistracy specially included, to be subservient to Him in promoting the interests of His Church—His kingdom in the world. And from that great doctrine flows the duty of nations and their rulers to own the kingdom of Christ and to advance its interests. Wherever the light of Revelation comes this duty is obligatory, at all times and in all circumstances. The two doctrines are brought before us in the Scriptures as closely related. As for instance, in the following passages: "And hath put all things under His feet, and gave Him to be the Head of all things to the Church." "As thou hast given Him power over all flesh, that He should give eternal life to as many as Thou hast given Him." "All power is given unto Me in heaven and on earth. Go ye, therefore, and teach all nations." The meaning of these passages being, not that dominion is founded in grace, or that magistracy derives its origin from Christ as Mediator, but that magistracy, which is an ordinance of God, for the public good and His own glory, has been put in subjection under Christ, to be serviceable to Him in promoting the interests of His kingdom in the world. Our reforming fathers understood well the important relation in which the two doctrines stand to each other; and hence, in the preface to the Directory of Government by the Westminster divines, and approved by the General Assembly of our Church, the two doctrines are brought before us in their close and intimate relationship, as they are presented in the word of God. "Jesus Christ," say the Westminster divines, " upon whose shoulders the government is, whose name is called Wonderful, Counsellor, the mighty God, the everlasting Father, the Prince of Peace; of the increase of whose government and peace there shall be no end; who sits upon the throne of David, and upon his kingdom, to order it, and to establish it with judgment and justice, from henceforth, even for ever; having all power given unto Him in heaven and earth by the Father, who raised Him from the dead, and set Him at His own right hand, far above all principalities, and power, and might, and dominion, and every name that is named, not only in this world, but also in that which is to come, and put all things under His feet, and gave Him to be the Head over all things to the Church, which is His body, the fulness of Him that filleth all in all: He being ascended up far above all heavens, that He might fill all things, received gifts for His Church, and gave officers necessary for the edification of His Church, and perfecting of His saints."

From the beginning of her history, the Reformed Church of Scotland evinced the greatest solicitude to distinguish between the civil and ecclesiastical jurisdictions; and to her sense of the great importance of having "the marches ridd between them" was owing, in a great measure, her spiritual independence; while the viewing of these jurisdictions as *collateral*, and not *co-ordinate* and distinct, and the union of them in the person of the Sovereign, formed the greatest barrier to the scriptural reformation of the Church of England. It has been justly said by Rowe, when speaking of the Reformation in Scotland, "That the Reformation of Religion came in otherwise to Scotland than in other parts, because the Queen, who then had the autoritie, being a malicious enemie to God's truth, thought that she should suppresse the Protestants in this kingdome by the bringing in of Frenchmen to help the Papists, who were upon her syde. Yet the Lord disappoynted her; and she dieing, the work of Reformation prospered ; and the ministers that were took not their pattern from any Kirk in the world; no, not fra Geneva itself; but laying God's word before them, made Reformation according thereunto, both in doctrine first and then in discipline, when and as they might get it overtaken. But in other places (as England) the Reformation coming in by the autoritie of the magistrate, nothing could be gotten done but according to the magistrat's desire; whilk hes been the cause why other kirks, professing the same trueth with us, yet had never the sinceritie of discipline amongst them, whilk is the thing that verie few magistrats or great personages (who would have absolute and unlimited autoritie and power to doe what they will, both in the State tyrannicallie, and in the Kirk Antichristianlyke) can away with."*

The desire on the part of the Church to have the sphere of the civil and ecclesiastical jurisdictions clearly defined was not peculiar to the period of the second Reformation. The illustrious men

* Rowe's History, Wodrow Society Ed., p. 12.

who were honoured by God to lay the foundations of the Church at the first Reformation were not insensible to its importance, because they felt that without "the marches" between the two jurisdictions "being ridd," the spiritual independence of the Church could not be maintained. The right of the Church to call and hold Assemblies they firmly insisted on; and while Knox and his brother Reformers maintained and taught that the Civil Magistrate had important duties to discharge *circa sacra*, such as protecting, defending, and fostering the Church, they would tolerate no jurisdiction or authority *in sacris;* and hence the noble declaration of Knox, in writing to the people of England from Geneva, in 1559, "*That if the king would usurp any other authority in God's religion than becometh a member of Christ's body, that first he be admonished according to God's word; and after, if he contemn the same, that he be subject to the yoke of discipline,* to whom they—the ministers—shall boldly say, as Azariah the High Priest said unto Uzziah, King of Judah, 'It is not lawful for thee, Uzziah, to offer incense, but it appertaineth to the priests, the sons of Aaron, who are consecrated to burn it: pass out, therefore, for thou hast offended, which thing shall not redound to thy glory.'"

In the General Assembly of 1565, Sessio 4^{to,} the Church, while remitting civil things to the magistrates, asserted her right to try, in the Ecclesiastical Courts, those guilty of adultery, &c. &c., and "to purge herself of all sic notorious malefactors."

The views which the early Reformers held on the subject of the jurisdiction of the Church and of the State, respectively, were afterwards clearly and fully embodied in the Second Book of Discipline, in the following among other propositions :—

"The Kirk, in the last sence, has a certean powar granted be God, according to the quhilk it uses a propre jurisdiction and government exercit to the comfort of the haill Kirk. This powar ecclesiastical is a powar and authoritie granted be God the Father, throw the Mediator, Jesus Chryst, unto sic wha has the speciall government of the Kirk committed to them, be lawfull calling, according to the word of God.

"The polecie of the Kirk, flowing from this powar, is an ordour or form of spirituall government, exercit be the members apointed thairto be the word of God, giffen be Chryst unto His office-bearers, to be usit for the weill of the haill bodie of the Kirk.

.   .   .   .

"This power and policie ecclesiasticall is different and distant in the awin nature fra that power and polecie quhilk is callet civill, aperteinand to the civill government of the comoun-weill; albeit they be bathe of God, and tend to a end, giff they be rightly usit; to wit, to advance the glore of God, and to haiff guid subjects.

"For this powar ecclesiasticall flowes immediately from God, throw the Mediator, Jesus Chryst, and is spirituall, nocht haiffing a temporall head on erthe, bot only Chryst, the spirituall King and Governor of His Kirk, now in glorie within the heavenes, at the right hand of His Fathar.

"Therefor, this powar and polecie of the Kirk sould lein upon the Word immediatlie, as the onlie ground thairof, and sould be takin from the pure fonteans of the Scripture; heiring the voice of Chryst, the onlie King of his Kirk; and therefor sche sould be rewlit be his lawes allcanerlie. It is a tytle falslie usurpit be Antechryst, to call himselff Head of the Kirk, and aught nocht to be attrebutit to angele or man, of what esteat soever he be, saving to Chryst Jesus, the onlie Head and Monarche of His Kirk.

. . . . .

"The civill power is callit the Powar of the Sword; the uther is callit the Power of the Keyes."

In 1582 the General Assembly transmitted the following remonstrance to the King, viz.:—That your Majesty, by advice of some counsellors, is taught to take upon your Grace that spiritual power and authority which properly belongs to Christ as only King and Head of the Kirk, the ministry and execution thereof to such as bear office in the ecclesiastical government of the same; so that in your Grace's person some men preases to erect ane new Popedome as though your Majesty could not be full king and head of this Commonwealth unless alsewell the spiritual as temporal sword be put in your hand—unless Christ be bereft of His authoritie and the two jurisdictions confounded which God has divided, which directly tends to the wrack of all true religion." In the same Assembly (Sessio 16) the following article, among others, was read and allowed, "as meit to be proponit. 1. Seeing the spiritual jurisdiction and government of the Kirk is granted be God the Father throw our Mediator, Jesus Christ, and given only to them that preaching, teaching, and overseeing, bear office within the same, to be exercised not be the injunctions of men, but be the only rule of God's Word. That the Act of Parliament concerning the liberty and jurisdiction of the Kirk be so plainly declared and enlarged that hereafter none other of whatsoever degree, or under whatsoever pretence, have any colour to ascribe or take upon them any part thereof, either in placing or displacing of ministers of God's Word in spiritual livings or offices, without the Kirk's admission, or in stopping the mouths of preachers, or putting them to silence, or taking upon them the judgment in trial of doctrine, or in hindering, staying, or disannulling the censures of the Kirk, or exempting any offender therefrom."

The same doctrine was taught and contended for by Henderson, Gillespie, and all the worthies of the second Reformation. And upon the accession of Charles II., the Scottish Parliament resolved—Act. xv., 7th February, 1659—that, before accepting the King, he should agree "that all matters civil be determined by the Parliaments of this kingdom, and all ecclesiastic matters by the General Assembly of this Kirk."

Had the doctrine so clearly laid down in the Second Book of Discipline, and in the Thirtieth Chapter of the Confession of Faith—these great authorised "subordinate standards" of the Church of Scotland—been adhered to, instead of being set aside and trampled under foot, the memorable Disruption of 1843 could not possibly have taken place.

In England matters were widely different. Instead of the marches between the civil and ecclesiastical judicatories being ridd, the Sovereign claimed the exercise of both, and, in repudiating the jurisdiction and universal headship of the Pope, assumed the title of Supreme Head of the Church for himself. A certain amount of resistance was for a time presented by the clergy to the assumption of so sacred a title; but at length the Convocation of Canterbury, and subsequently the Convocation of York, agreed to admit the claim and accept the title, with the reservation proposed by Archbishop Warham—*quantum per legem Christi licet* (so far as the law of Christ permits)—a qualification which, when proposed, was offensive to Henry, but which was afterwards accepted by him on being reminded that after he had succeeded in finally settling matters with the Pope the restrictive provision could easily be repealed.

That the early Reformers of the Church of England would have ordered matters otherwise than was done is evident from their writings. Indeed, there was no material difference as regards either doctrine or discipline between the views entertained by them and by the continental and Scotch Reformers; but they found it impossible to overcome the repugnance of Henry, and afterwards of Elizabeth, to a Church possessing independent jurisdiction in spiritual matters.

What can be more distinct, in regard to the sole Headship of Christ as respects the Church, which is His Body, than the following article, from "*the Confession of England,*" inserted in Jewell's Apology (1562) :—

"Art. 4. We believe that there is one Church of God; ..... and that this Church is the Kingdom, the Body, and the Spouse of Christ; that Christ ALONE is the Prince of this Kingdom; that Christ ALONE is the Head of this Body; and that Christ ALONE is the Bridegroom of this Spouse."

Latimer, who possessed in a great degree that fearlessness which was so characteristic of John Knox, laid down, clearly and boldly, in his discourses before the King and the Court, the line of demarcation between the civil and ecclesiastical jurisdiction, insisting on the necessity of carefully keeping them distinct, and warning them to beware "of making a mingle-mangle of them," a warning the neglect of which has been most disastrous to the Church of England.

In the Thirty-seventh Article of the Church of England the following clause of limitation was inserted :—

"Whereas we attribute to the Queen's Majesty

the chief government, by which titles we understand the minds of some slanderous folks to be offended; we give not to our princes the ministering either of God's Word or of the Sacraments, the which thing the Injunctions also lately set forth by Elizabeth our Queen do most plainly testify: but that only prerogative which we see to have been given always to all godly princes in holy Scriptures by God Himself; that is, that they should rule all estates and degrees committed to their charge by God, whether they be ecclesiastical or temporal, and restrain with the civil sword the stubborn and evil-doers."

The clause in "the Injunctions" referred to in the Thirty-seventh Article is as follows:—"And further, her Majesty forbiddeth all manner her subjects to give ear or credit to such perverse and malicious persons, which most sinisterly and maliciously labour to notifie to her loving subjects, how by words of the said Oath (*the Oath of Allegiance to her Majesty*) it may be collected, that the Kings or Queens of this Realm, possessors of the Crown, may challenge authority and power of Ministry of divine service in the Church, wherein her said subjects be much abused by such evil-disposed persons. For certainly her Majesty neither doth nor ever will challenge any authority than that was challenged and lately used by the said noble Kings of famous memory, King Henry the Eighth and King Edward the Sixth, which is and was of ancient time due to the Imperial Crown of this Realm, that is, under God to have the sovereignty and rule over ALL MANNER OF PERSONS born within these her realms, dominions, and countries, of what estate, either Ecclesiastical or Temporal soever they be, so as no other foreign power shall or ought to have any superiority over them. And if any person that hath conceived any other sense of the form of the said Oath, shall accept the same Oath WITH THIS INTERPRETATION, sense, or meaning, her Majesty is well pleased to accept every such in that behalf, as her good and obedient subjects, and shall acquit them of all manner of penalties contained in the said Act, against such as shall peremptorily or obstinately take the same Oath."

The Irish Articles are still more explicit, inasmuch as the qualifying or limiting clause extends to and includes, not only doctrine, but also *government* and *discipline*. It is thus expressed:—

"The King's Majesty, under God, hath the sovereign and chief power, within his realms and dominions, over all manner of persons, of what estate, either ecclesiastical or civil, soever they be; so as no other foreign powers hath or ought to have any superiority over them.

"We do profess that the supreme government of all estates within the said realms and dominions, in all causes, as well ecclesiastical as temporal, doth of right appertain to the King's Highness. Neither do we give unto him hereby the administration of the Word and Sacraments, OR THE POWER OF THE KEYS; but the prerogative only, which we see to have been always given unto all godly princes in holy Scripture by God himself; that is, that he should contain all estates and degrees committed to his charge by God, whether they be ecclesiastical or civil, within their duty, and restrain the stubborn and evil-doers with the power of the civil sword."

In his *Aaron's Rod Blossoming,* when discoursing of the power and privilege of the magistrate in things and causes ecclesiastical—what it is not, and what it is—Gillespie cites the Articles of the Irish Church in support of his argument against the Erastians, and refers to them as "Articles of Faith famous among orthodox and learned men in these kingdoms," and which "do plainly exclude the magistrate from the administration of the Word and Sacraments, *and from the power of the keys of the kingdom of heaven.*"*

To these Articles the Westminster Assembly were probably more indebted than to any other compendium of Christian doctrine. Ussher, who was second to no theologian of his time, and who then, as Archbishop of Armagh, presided over the Irish Church, had clear views in regard to the line of demarcation between the civil and spiritual jurisdictions. These are brought out with great distinctness in his speech, delivered in the Castle Chamber of Dublin, concerning the Oath of Supremacy, in the following passage (pp. 3, 4, 5):—"God, for the better settling of piety and honesty among men, and the repressing of profaneness and other vices, hath established two dis-

* Aaron's Rod Blossoming, Chap. viii.

tinct powers upon the earth: the one of the *keys* committed to the Church; the other of the *sword*, committed to the Civil Magistrate. That of the *keys* is ordained to work upon the inward man, having immediate relation to the remitting or retaining of sins, (John xx. 23.) That of the sword is appointed to work upon the outward man: yielding protection to the obedient, and inflicting external punishment upon the rebellious and disobedient. .... When St Peter, that had the *keys* committed unto him, made bold to draw the *sword*, he was commanded to put it up (Matt. xxvi. 52), as a weapon he had no authority to meddle withal. And on the other side, when Uzziah the king would venture upon the execution of the priest's office, it was said unto him, "It pertaineth not unto thee, Uzziah, to burn incense unto the Lord, but to the priests the sons of Aaron, that are consecrated to burn incense," (2 Chron. xxvi. 18.) Let this, therefore, be our second conclusion: that the power of the sword and of the keys *are two distinct ordinances of God; and that the prince hath no more authority to enter upon the execution of any part of the priest's function than the priest has to intrude upon any part of the office of the prince."*

It is evident, from Cranmer's examination before Brokes, Bishop of Gloucester, the Pope's sub-delegate, that he understood the title "Supreme Head of the Church," in the sense in which Owen explains and defends it in his animadversions on a treatise entitled *Fiat Lux*,* viz., as excluding the jurisdiction of any and all foreign potentates, and especially as against the Pope's claim to universal headship and supremacy.

During his examination, Cranmer was interrogated thus by Dr Martin, one of the King's Commissioners :—

Martin—Now, sir, touching the last part of your oration, you denied that the Pope's Holiness was supreme head of the Church of Christ.

Cranmer—I did so.

Martin—Who say you, then, is supreme head.

Cranmer—Christ.

Martin—But whom hath Christ left here in earth His vicar and head of His Church?

Cranmer—Nobody.

Martin—Ah! Why told you not King Henry this, when you made him supreme head? And now nobody is. This is treason against his own person, as you then made him.

Cranmer—I mean not but every king in his own realm and dominion is supreme head, and so was he supreme head of the Church of Christ in England.

Martin—Is this always true? And was it ever so in Christ's Church?

Cranmer—It was so.

. . . . .

After this, Dr Martin demanded of him, Who was supreme head of the Church of England? "Marry,"

* The production of Cane, a Franciscan Friar.

quoth my lord of Canterbury, "Christ is the head of this member, so He is of the whole body of the universal Church." "Why," quoth Dr Martin, "you made King Henry VIII. supreme head of the Church." "Yea," said the Archbishop, "of all the PEOPLE of England, as well ecclesiastical as temporal." "And not of the Church?" said Martin. "No," said he; "for Christ is only head of His Church, and of the faith and religion of the same. The king is head and governor of his people, which are the visible church." "What!" quoth Martin, "you never durst tell the king so." "Yes, that I durst," quoth he, "and did, in the publication of his style, wherein he was named supreme head of the Church; there was never other thing meant."

It must, however, be admitted that, in Cranmer's replies before the Council, there is, to say the least of it, a seeming inconsistency. Certainly they are not for a moment to be compared to the manly and unmistakeable utterances of Alexander Henderson, in his correspondence with Charles I., when he says, "Such an headship as the kings of England have claimed, and such a supremacy as the two Houses of Parliament crave, with the appeals from the supreme ecclesiastical judicatory to them, as set over the Church in the same line of subordination, I do utterly disclaim, upon such reasons as give myself satisfaction; although no man shall be more willing to submit to civil powers, each one in their own place, and more unwilling to make any trouble than myself."

In the same letter Henderson gives his Majesty to understand that he was far from being satisfied with the condition of the Church of England. "Learned men," he says, "have observed many defects in the Reformation of the Church of England, as, that it hath not perfectly purged out the Roman leaven; that it hath depraved the discipline of the Church, by conforming it to the civil policy; that it hath added many Church offices higher and lower than those instituted by the Son of God, which is as unlawful as to take away offices warranted by the Divine Institution, and other the like, which have moved some to apply this saying to the Church of England, *Multi ad perfectionem pervenirent, nisi jam se pervenisse crederent.*"*

As originally put forward by Henry, and reasserted by Elizabeth, the claim to supremacy over the Church proved a stumbling-block to not a few of the clergy. And in order to meet the scruples known to be entertained by many, the "Injunctions of Queen Elizabeth" (already referred to), containing limitations similar to those embodied in the Articles, and explaining the modified sense in which the doctrine of the Royal Supremacy over the Church was to be understood, were issued, and instead of the phrase, "the Supreme Head of the Church," the expression "Supreme or Chief Governor" was substituted. Had "the Queen's Injunctions," and the limiting clause in Article 37, been held and declared by formal legal authoritative enactment as qualifying

* Second Letter to Charles I.

the doctrine of the Royal Supremacy to the extent specified by John Livingstone in his examination before the Council at Edinburgh, in December 1662; and had the right of the Church to call and hold her councils and assemblies, irrespective of "the commandment and will of princes," been admitted and secured, along with the proper representation of the congregations in the Church Courts, however much Presbyterians might disapprove of her form of government, they would doubtless be disposed to admit that the Erastianism of the Church of England was well-nigh cast out of her; but the melancholy fact is, that "the Queen's Injunctions," and the limiting clause in Article 37 were practically inoperative, of no real value, altogether powerless in delivering the Church from the Erastian grasp of the sovereign, by which she is rendered utterly helpless in determining matters of doctrine, discipline, and government; cannot possibly reform herself, has no power to separate the lepers from the clean; and therefore the only possible remedy is to root up the doctrine of the Royal Supremacy, *as far as matters spiritual are concerned*, as a tree not of God's planting but of man's, whose fruit has been evil, and that continually, and thus, by unqualified abolition, to make a clean sweep of it. Nothing can be more deplorable than the present condition of the Church of England. We have the melancholy spectacle presented of the Evangelical clergy clinging to the doctrine of the Royal Supremacy—in other words, Erastianism in its grossest form—as their very salvation. We have the Ritualists, on the one hand, transforming her into a vast recruiting establishment for the Church of Rome; and we have the Rationalists, or Broad Church party, on the other, endeavouring to turn her into a huge Noah's Ark, whose excellency is reckoned in proportion to its capacity to receive beasts clean and unclean alike; to receive into its comprehensive embrace ministers and members of all varieties of doctrinal views and opinions, allowing each and all to disport themselves according to their pleasure, unrestrained by any fear whatever of creeds or confessions.

When Livingstone was before the Council at Edinburgh, the Lord Chancellor addressed him thus:—
"The Council looks on you as a suspect person, and therefore thinks it fitting to require you to take the oath of alleadgeance. You know it and have considered it?

Mr Livingstone—Yes, my Lord.

Lord Chan. — The Clerk will read it to you. (He reads it.) Now that you have heard it read, are you free to take the oath?

Mr Livingstone—My Lord, I doe acknowledge the King's Majesty (whose person and government I wish God to bless) to be the only lawful supreame Magistrate of this and all other of His Majesty's dominions, and that His Majesty is the supreame civill governour over all persons and in all causes, as well ecclesiastick as civill; but for the oath as it stands in terms, I am not free to take it.

Lord Chan.—I think you and we agree as to the oath?

Lord Advocate—My Lord Chancellor, Your Lordship doth not observe that he useth a distinction that the King is the supreame civill governour that he may make way for the co-ordinate power of the Presbyterie.

When before the Council, John Livingstone gave ample evidence that he knew well how to "ridd the marches between the civil and ecclesiastical jurisdictions"—in other words, how to render to Cæsar the things which are Cæsar's, and to God the things which are God's. This he did by two clear and distinct declarations:—

1. "My Lord, I doe indeed believe and confess that Jesus Christ is the only Head of His Church, and that He only hath power to appoint a government and discipline for removing of offences in His (own) house, which is not dependent upon civil powers, and nowayes wrongs civil powers. But withall, I acknowledge His Majesty to have a cumulative power and inspection in the house of God for seeing both the tables of the law keeped; and that His Majesty hath all the ordinary power that was in the kings of Israel and Judah, and in the Christian emperors and kings since the primitive times, for reforming, *according to the Word*, what is amiss."

2. "I have always been of that judgment, and am, and will be, that His Majesty is supream governour, *in a civil way*, over all persons and in all causes."

I have said that the melancholy fact is that the

limiting clause in Article 37 relative to the Royal Supremacy has been practically useless. A far more melancholy fact, however, is that the doctrine of the Royal Supremacy, which originally was so distasteful to many of the clergy—against which they protested as an invasion of the prerogative of Christ, the great and only Head of the Church; which was submitted to in hope of being able at some future time to obtain such modifications as would bring the doctrine into harmony with the Scriptures; which many of them interpreted as binding them to nothing more than a repudiation of the jurisdiction and headship of the Pope—is now clung to by the Evangelical party in the Church of England as their defence and glory, the corner-stone on which the Church, as established by law, not only rests, but ought to rest, as its legitimate and desirable basis.

A great deal has been said of late about the recent celebrated utterance of a well-known statesman on the doctrine of the Royal Supremacy; but we need not be surprised to find statesmen coming forth thus to defend Erastianism in its grossest forms, when such men as Dr H. M'Neile, formerly of Liverpool, now Dean of Ripon, not only cling to the Royal Supremacy, but pronounce glowing panegyrics upon it as the "GRAND DEFENCE" of England. "The history of England," says Dr M'Neile, "since her grand protest and separation, supplies a bright contrast (to the Papal nations); and if, through overweening pride in her supposed indefeasible liberties and unarrestible progress, she removes her GRAND DEFENCE—THE ROYAL SUPREMACY IN ALL CAUSES, ECCLESIASTICAL AS WELL AS CIVIL—she will, in my opinion, imperil the very privileges she now idolises, and supply another illustration of the sacred proverb that pride goeth before a fall."

That the doctrine of the Royal Supremacy should exercise such a lamentable influence over the minds of such men as Dr M'Neile is one of the strongest evidences of its seductive and blinding effects upon those who have been brought up under its baleful shadow. How the spiritual independence of the Church can be best secured is a question of the greatest importance. During the Ten Years' Conflict, those who constituted the majority of the Church of Scotland, and contended for her independence when imperilled, were told, both by the Court of Session and by leading members of her Majesty's Government and of the Opposition, that in order to obtain the spiritual freedom struggled for, those who valued it ought to retire from the Establishment, and occupy the platform on which the dissenting and non-Established Churches stood, as by so doing the independence in spiritual matters which they insisted on could alone be enjoyed; but several years after, views the very opposite were proclaimed from the same bench of the Court of Session, and it was boldly stated, in the most unqualified terms, that no such independence could in any case be conceded; that the Established Church possessed no intrinsic jurisdiction in spiritual matters, but solely by derivation from the State; while non-established Churches, having had no jurisdiction, either civil or spiritual, conferred by the State, were without any such authority at all, being mere voluntary associations, whose proceedings were liable to be reviewed by the Civil Courts equally as those of any society, club, or coterie in the kingdom.

It has generally been taken for granted that all Erastian control on the part of the State would cease were establishments of religion to be abolished. This, however, is a mere assumption. Were there no Established Churches in the land, the question would still remain,—What standing is the Church of Christ entitled to among the nations of the earth, and how is her spiritual independence to be acknowledged and maintained? Principles have been laid down by our judges on the bench, as for instance in the Culsalmond case, previous to the Disruption of 1843, and in the Cardross case, after the Disruption, which would warrant the interference of civil rulers with any Church whatever, whether Established or non-Established. The mere disappearance of an Establishment is no security whatever, in or by itself, that the Church which has been disestablished shall be secure in the enjoyment of spiritual freedom. This has been well put by Dr Buchanan in his admirable " History of the Ten Years' Conflict."*

" The ground that the Church has received a civil

---

* Ten Years' Conflict, vol. i., p. 21.

establishment is by no means the only one on which the State may claim a right to control her spiritual freedom. Nor is it the simple renunciation of such an establishment that will suffice to protect the Church from the encroachments and usurpation of the civil power. The only ground on which the Church can have any real security for the permanent maintenance of her peculiar rights and liberties, is the recognition by the State of those fundamental principles evolved in the preceding summary, as being inherent in the very essence of the Church—as entering into its very constitution as a divine society, a kingdom not of this world. Let these be acknowledged, and then, whether established or unestablished, the Church will be left to act within her own province, undisturbed by external assaults; but let these fundamental principles be denied, or not admitted, and the want of an establishment will be no protection whatever against the invasions of the secular government."

Had the spirit of Cranmer, Latimer, Ridley, Hooper, Jewel, &c., continued to influence and direct the movements of the Church of England, we cannot but believe, taking into account the advances which have been made since their days in civil liberty, that matters, as respects spiritual freedom, would now be far different. The keys which the Head of the Church, as Master in His own house, committed to His servants before ascending to the upper sanctuary—to be used by them during his bodily absence for certain purposes defined by His

Word, that His House might be preserved free from all unauthorized intrusion, and his worship kept sacred and entire, instead of carefully guarding, they have sinfully surrendered, unto the hands of those who have no right whatever to their possession, keys, sooner than surrender which, our covenanting forefathers yielded up their lives. Hence the noble testimony of brave old Cargill, in his last speech on the scaffold—" As to the causes of my suffering, the chief is not acknowledging the present authority as it is established in the supremacy and explanatory act. This is the magistracy I have rejected—that which is invested with Christ's power. Seeing that power taken from Christ, which is His glory, and made the essential of an earthly crown, seemed to me as if one were wearing my husband's garments after he had killed him."

Since the above was written, the debate on the doctrine of the Royal Supremacy, in connection with the consideration of the Bill for disestablishing the Irish Church, has taken place in the House of Commons.

There can be no doubt that, as far as the application of the doctrine to the United Church of England and Ireland is concerned, that the exposition given by Sir Roundell Palmer is historically correct; while that given by Mr Disraeli and Dr Ball evinced defective knowledge of the principle which they professed to state and defend. Sir Roundell Palmer, however, introduced another principle, which lays the Church entirely at the mercy of the Sovereign, viz., the Erastian controlling power, which he insisted on as a necessary condition of the State consenting to establish the Church — the *Church's Freedom* being the price of the *Church's Establishment*. The Church of Scotland has always not only admitted but asserted the supremacy of the Sovereign over all *Persons* in the realm, ecclesiastics not less than civilians, and also the right of dealing with and deciding all ecclesiastical questions in which the destination of property is the primary element involved, as far as said destination is concerned; but the right of the Civil Courts to interfere with her decisions in spiritual matters she has never conceded; and when, in 1843, in violation alike— as she believed then, and believes still—of Scriptural principle, constitutional privilege, and legal right, an attempt was made to deprive her of her spiritual freedom, rather than consent to surrender it, she renounced the benefits of an Establishment, and, under protest that she had been unrighteously dealt with as respects the liberty wherewith she had been invested by her great Head, and which was solemnly guaranteed to her by the law of the land, withdrew from connexion with the State to execute, as best she might, by the blessing of her *Divine and only Head*, the great commission with which He had charged her.

It is evident that Mr Disraeli and Dr Ball grounded their views mainly upon what is expressed in the 37th Article, overlooking the limitations relative thereto, set forth in the " Injunctions of

Queen Elizabeth." Of the 37th Article, as it at present stands, I do not, of course, approve; but at the same time I believe that as formidable a barrier, to say the least of it, to the Scriptural Reformation of the Church of England is reared by the 21st Article, which declares that "General Councils may not be gathered together WITHOUT THE COMMANDMENT AND WILL OF PRINCES." There can be little hope for a Church in such circumstances. Mr Disraeli seems to imagine that such a prohibitory power on the part of the Sovereign is one of the guarantees for purity of doctrine. Had he affirmed the contrary, he would have been nearer the truth.* Our own great Reformer, John Knox, and his noble associates, understood this well, when they said, "Take away from us the FREEDOM OF OUR ASSEMBLIES, and you take away the blessed evangel."

The only man, perhaps, whose opinion *as a lawyer* as to the real meaning and bearing of the doctrine of the Supremacy of the Crown is entitled to rank along with that given by Sir Roundell Palmer is

* The utter helplessness of the Church of England in this respect may be shown by the case of Whiston, a Professor of Mathematics at Cambridge. The Convocation met to consider his case in 1711. They found him guilty of "several damnable and blasphemous assertions against the doctrine of the ever blessed Trinity," and accordingly condemned his doctrine with a view to befitting censure. But the Queen refused to ratify their judgment, and the consequence was that they were utterly helpless, while the heretic, having had the shield of the Sovereign cast over him, defied them. Judge Hale lays down the law relating to the Church of England as follows:—"If ecclesiastical laws are not confirmed by Parliament, the king may revoke and annul them at pleasure."

L

Lord Cairns. Of his great ability and strict conscientiousness no one can for a moment entertain a doubt, but in regard to this particular question he may, unconsciously, have a bias. When the bill reaches the House of Lords, it will be interesting to have his exposition of the *Article* relative to the Royal Supremacy; but we believe that it will be difficult for him, consistently with the history of the doctrine, to give any exposition of it substantially different from that of Sir Roundell Palmer.

We pronounce no opinion here on the question of the disestablishment of the Irish Church; but, apart from that question altogether, it is truly sad to see men like Dr Ball insisting and demanding that the grasp of the Sovereign, which has so long prevented anything like freedom of action on the part of the Church, shall on no account be relaxed, when the *Articles of the Irish Church*, which were mainly drawn up by the greatest theologian who has ever adorned her, expressly denies to the Sovereign the right of ordering the *doctrine* or administering the discipline and *government* of the Church—the right, not only of the ministry of the Word, but also of "THE POWER OF THE KEYS."

APPENDIX.

PROPOSED CORPORATE RE-UNION

OF THE

ROMAN CATHOLIC, GREEK, AND ANGLICAN CHURCHES.

THE Association for promoting the union of Christendom was originated in the year 1857. "On the Feast of the Nativity of the Blessed Virgin Mary" (I quote from the preface to a volume of sermons, "printed for certain members of the Association,") certain Roman Catholics, Greeks, and Anglicans met in the parish of St Clement Danes, Strand, in the City of Westminster—having that morning previously, at their respective altars, asked Almighty God's blessing upon their contemplated plans;—and, after duly arranging its organisation, and drawing up the well-known Paper of the Association, thirty-four persons formally enrolled themselves members. A DIGNITARY OF THE SCOTTISH EPISCOPAL CHURCH WAS IN THE CHAIR. The following resolution was moved by a distinguished Roman Catholic layman, seconded by a well-known clergyman of the Church of England, supported by members of the Greek Church and others, and was unanimously adopted :—

"That a Society, to be called the Association for the promoting the Unity of Christendom, be now formed, for united prayer that visible unity may be restored to Christendom; and that the Paper now before this meeting be sanctioned, printed, and circulated, as the basis upon which this Society desires to act."

Since that day, the Association has steadily increased, as will be seen from the following statement :—

On September 8, 1858, a year after its formation, there had enrolled themselves members, ... 675
On September 8, 1859 (in addition), . . . 833
     ,,   1860   ,,   . . . 1060
     ,,   1861   ,,   . . . 1007
     ,,   1862   ,,   . . . 1393
     ,,   1863   ,,   . . . 1202
     ,,   1864   ,,   . . . 929[*]

Thus making a total of . . . 7099

Of these the great majority are members of the Church of England; but there are nearly a thousand belonging to the Latin Communion, and about three

[*] The record for 1864 is incomplete, many of the returns not having been received when the above list was made out.

hundred members of the Eastern Church. The Paper of the Association has been translated into Latin, French, Greek, and Italian, and sent abroad in various ways and by different channels. Local secretaries, both at home and in foreign countries, are being increased, and many correspondents are labouring energetically, and with considerable success in the cause. The Association has been approved in the highest ecclesiastical quarters, both amongst Latins, Anglicans, and Greeks. THE HOLY FATHER GAVE HIS BLESSING TO THE SCHEME WHEN FIRST STARTED, AND REPEATED THAT BLESSING WITH A DIRECT AND KINDLY COMMENDATION TO ONE OF THE ENGLISH SECRETARIES, WHO WAS MORE RECENTLY GRANTED THE HONOUR OF A SPECIAL INTERVIEW. The ex-Patriarch of Constantinople, and other Eastern Prelates, have approved of the Association, and so likewise have several Bishops, both Anglican and Roman Catholic, in England, Ireland, and SCOTLAND, as well as on the Continent and in America.

To the volume of Sermons "by members of the Association," being "members also of the Roman Catholic, Oriental, and Anglican Communions," is prefixed the following dedication to the

"Most Blessed and most Holy Father in Christ, the Pope;" the most Blessed and most Holy Father in Christ, the Archbishop and Patriarch of Constantinople, and the most Honourable and most Reverend Father in Christ, the Archbishop of Canterbury, " in hope of the future Union of the flock of Christ, and of the universal diffusion of the Catholic Faith throughout the whole world."

BEATISSIMO, ET SANCTISSIMO IN CHRISTO PATRI
PIO,
DIVINA PROVIDENTIA,
PAPÆ NONO,
S. SEDIS APOSTOLICÆ EPISCOPO;
NECNON
BEATISSIMO ET SANCTISSIMO IN CHRISTO PATRI,
SOPHRONIO,
ARCHIEPISCOPO CONSTANTINOPOLITANO,
NOVÆ ROMÆ PATRIARCHÆ ŒCUMENICO;
SED ET
HONORATISSIMO ET REVERENDISSIMO IN CHRISTO PATRI,
CAROLO THOMÆ,
ARCHIEPISCOPO CANTUARIENSI,
TOTIUS ANGLIÆ PRIMATI,
IN SPEM UNIONIS FUTURÆ GREGIS CHRISTI,
HEU! TAM DIU IN SEIPSO PARTITI,
ET IN EXPECTATIONE UNIVERSALIS FIDEI CATHOLICÆ
PER TOTUM ORBEM DIFFUSIONIS,
QUAM CONCEDAT DOMINUS DEUS OMNIPOTENS.
AMEN.

The Association has thus received the blessing of the Holy Father, the Pope,—the approval of the ex-Patriarch of Constantinople, and other Eastern Prelates, as well as of several Bishops, both Anglican and Roman Catholic, in our own and other countries; while, at the meeting at which it "was originated," and its organisation arranged, "A DIGNITARY OF THE SCOTTISH EPISCOPAL CHURCH WAS IN THE CHAIR. Each member of the Association is to pray daily "for the Corporate Re-Union" of these three great bodies which claim for themselves "the inheritance of the

Priesthood and the name Catholic," and in addition to daily prayer for the above object, each Priest comes under an "obligation" to offer, "at least once in three months, the Holy Sacrifice for the same intention." *

Associations which seem more befitting a Popish than a Protestant Church, are becoming numerous in the Church of England. Take two of them by way of illustration.

First, "The Confraternity of the Blessed Sacrament of the Body and Blood of Christ."

This "Confraternity was inaugurated on the first Thursday in Advent 1862, to consist of Bishops, Priests, and Deacons, and members of Brotherhoods and Sisterhoods, and Communicants of both sexes being in communion with the Church of England."

The objects of the Association are—

"1. The honour due to the Person of our LORD JESUS CHRIST in the Blessed Sacrament of His Body and Blood. 2. Mutual and special intercession at the time of, and in union with, the Eucharistic sacrifice.

"The Superior General, the Superiors of Wards, and certain Priests-associate, annually elected, form the Council."

The doctrine taught may be judged of from the title of the sermon which was preached before the Confraternity on the occasion of the first anniversary. It is as follows:—"The Union of the Natural and Supernatural Substances in the Holy Eucharist, analogous to that of the Human and Divine Natures in the Incarnation."

---

* The Pope has since, we believe, withdrawn from the Association the light of his countenance.

APPENDIX.

The other Association to which I refer is called the Society or Company of the Love of Jesus.

Eleven Addresses were delivered before the Society by Dr Pusey during "A Retreat," the subject of the last Address being on "Prayers for departed Companions of the Society."

To the Address Dr Pusey has prefixed the following dedication :—

"To the Foundress of the Society of the Holy Trinity and of the Company of the Love of Jesus, and, under God, the Restorer, after three centuries, of the religious life in the English Church, with the prayer that the work of love for souls which she has so manifoldly designed, and in which she has so unceasingly laboured, may be to her endless bliss as to the glory of the Redeemer, and that the prayers which she has caused to be multiplied may return into her own bosom."

Well may we ask,—Where is all this to end? How pitiful to see a man of Dr Pusey's talents and learning condescending to such miserable twaddle!

SANSON AND CO., PRINTERS, EDINBURGH.

www.ingramcontent.com/pod-product-compliance
Lightning Source LLC
Chambersburg PA
CBHW031448160426
43195CB00010BB/903